Bread

MACHINE
Cookbook

THE ULTIMATE, COMPLETE AND DELICIOUS 250 BREAD
MACHINE RECIPES COOKBOOK, FROM MAKING TO BAKING,
ALL YOU NEED TO KNOW ABOUT HOMEMADE BREAD IS HERE

Stephany L. Rosato

TABLE OF CONTENTS

INTRODUCTION

The bread machine, also popularly referred to as the bread maker, is a machine or appliance found in the kitchen created to bake raw ingredients into consumable bread. Bread is a type of food that is baked using a variety of dough and can be in so many different shapes and sizes and qualities. Bread ingredients are dependent on the needs of the one baking it and can be prepared in various methods. Bread is known to be one of the world's oldest foods.

A bread machine is made up of a bread pan and paddles built-in and placed in the middle of a multi-purpose oven that is small and manageable. This small oven has a built-in micro-computer, which is what you use to operate the bread maker. There are different settings on the bread maker, depending on the type of bread you intend to bake. These settings include those for white bread, whole bread, French bread, and simple dough like those of pizzas. There is also an option of a timer on the bread maker to automatically go on and off automatically even when you are not in the vicinity to operate it.

The bread maker is basically a smaller oven version that uses electricity and which can only accommodate one bread pan in it. The bread pan is characterized by an axle which is located at its bottom, connecting it to a motor, run by electricity. The waterproof axle then connects to a small metallic paddle. The paddle is the one that kneads the dough.

The bread maker has a lid that is either opaque or see-through, depending on the make and model. The lid also comes with a vent that is used to remove all the excess steam produced during the baking process and an air vent on its side to allow air to come in, which is vital for the dough to rise well. It has a control panel at the top that will enable you to operate it easily.

Advantages of Bread Machines

A bread machine does it all instead of you. This means you will be able to avoid kitchen mess, as the bread machine does everything from mixing to kneading to baking. Yes, it sounds like magic, but it is for real. Just imagine warm bread and a clean kitchen. Dreams can come true!

Bread machines keep your health under control. By this, we mean that you can choose the ingredients you want and create a bread that is carb-free and free of any additives that might cause harm to your body. This feature is very appreciated by those who follow the keto diet. You can make your own bread that is much better than the store-bought version, at a low cost, and you know it was created in a clean environment where cross-contamination is not possible.

A bread machine allows you to have fresh, warm bread every day. This is perhaps the most obvious benefit of a bread-making machine. Most bread machines have a time function you can set to have your bread ready at a certain time. This is very useful, as it allows you to prepare the ingredients and then continue with your daily chores, while the bread machine does everything else for you. Just imagine, you are coming home after an exhausting day of work, and warm, delicious bread is waiting for you!

Bread machines save money. Yes, bread machines may be expensive initially, but buying bread every day, or even just every week, is more costly. Not to mention all of that thrown away bread, the stale bread that no one wants to eat anymore. With each slice, you are throwing away your money. The bread machine maker allows you to make smaller or larger loaves and ones that fit your family's dietary and consumption habits. Besides, making bread from scratch is always cheaper than buying it at the store.

Bread machines produce better quality bread. Fresh bread is fresh bread, and no store-bought version can compete with that. In addition, what about that chewy, rubber-like bread you sometimes get? Something like that will never happen to you with a bread-making machine. The homemade bread is made with natural ingredients and does not have any artificial additives. The additives that are used in store-bought bread can keep it fresher for a longer time, but they affect the texture. It is always better to make bread fresh and additive-free than to eat "fake-fresh" bread for days.

Bread machines are easy to use. The bread machine looks like a simple appliance, and believe us, it is. If you are not good with the baking process and somehow you always end up with over- or under-cooked foods, you can skip this worry, as the bread-making machine bakes everything to perfection.

Bread making machines make more than bread. The bread machine can be used for many other purposes besides making bread. You can use it to make a baguette, sweet breads, and even dough. The possibilities are endless.

These are just some of the advantages of a bread machine. We are sure you will soon discover others and learn to appreciate the many uses of a bread machine. And while that happens, we suggest you enjoy our recipe collection from this book.

TRADITIONAL/CLASSIC BREAD

1. CIABATTA BREAD

PREPARATION	COOKING	SERVES
15 MIN	30-35 MIN	8

INGREDIENTS

- 1 1/2 cup water
- 1 1/2 teaspoon salt
- One teaspoon white sugar
- One tablespoon olive oil
- 3 1/4 cup bread flour
- 1 1/2 teaspoon bread machine yeast

DIRECTIONS

1. Mix all ingredients in your stand mixer but for olive oil. Mix with dough hook at low speed. Mix for 10 minutes. Scrape down the sides if necessary.
2. Add the olive oil and whisk for another 5 minutes.
3. The dough will be pretty sticky and wet; this is what you want, so you can avoid the desire to add more flour.
4. Put the dough on a kindly floured surface, cover it with a large bowl or oily plastic wrap then leave it for 15 minutes.
5. Dust Baking sheets with light flour, or cover them with parchment paper.
6. Divide the dough into two parts using a serrated knife and shape each piece into a 3×14-inch oval.
7. Place the loaves on prepared sheets and dust with flour.
8. Cover the dough loaves and leave it to rise for about 45 minutes at a draft-free spot.
9. Preheat oven to 425 F.
10. Spritz loaves with water.
11. In the oven, put loaves, placed on the middle rack.
12. Bake, for approximately 25 to 35 mins, until its color is golden brown.
13. Serve, and have fun.

NUTRITION

Carbohydrates 3 g
Fats 5.6 g
Protein 9.6 g
Calories 319

2. ZOJIRUSHI BREAD MACHINE LIGHT SOURDOUGH BREAD

PREPARATION	COOKING	SERVES
5 MIN	25 MIN	8

INGREDIENTS

Sourdough starter:

- Sourdough starter:
- 1 1/2 cups of water
- 2 cups (256 grams) of bread flour
- 2 tsp. of active dry yeast

Bread Ingredients:

- 3 tbsp. of apple cider vinegar
- 2 tbsp. of lemon juice
- 3 cups of bread flour
- 1 tsp. of fine sea salt
- 2 tsp. of active dry yeast

DIRECTIONS

1. Put the kneading blades in the Zojirushi Home Bakery Supreme bread machine; Place the pan of bread into the machine.
2. Add the bread flour and leaven in the bowl.
3. Set a "sourdough starter" course and press Start. It will take around 2 hours to complete.
4. The starting point is all bubbly.
5. For the bread:
6. Hit cancel to clear once the sourdough starter ends and beeps.
7. Add in the specified ingredients, with yeast placed on top of the flour.
8. Close the cover and set a "basic" sequence.
9. When the bread is baked (just 4 hours), pop out and knock out onto a cooling rack.
10. When cooled, the bread can be cut and frozen for long time storage.

NUTRITION

Carbohydrates 3 g
Fats 5.6 g
Protein 9.6 g
Calories 319

3. SOFTEST SOFT BREAD WITH AIR POCKETS USING BREAD MACHINE

PREPARATION	COOKING	SERVES
15 MIN	200 MIN	8

INGREDIENTS

- 1 cup of lukewarm (105 to 115 degrees F/40 to 45 degrees C)
- Four teaspoons of honey
- Two teaspoons of active dry yeast
- 2 cups of all-purpose flour
- Four teaspoons of olive oil
- 1/2 teaspoon of salt

DIRECTIONS

1. Put warm water into the bread machine pan and sprinkle honey in warm water until honey is dissolved. Add yeast to the mixture and let it sit for about 10 minutes before yeast begins to foam. In the manufacturer's suggested order, add flour, olive oil, and salt to the bread pan.
2. If the machine has that choice, select a soft setting; otherwise, set a standard-setting, and start the machine. Let the bread cool before slicing.

NUTRITION

Carbohydrates 3 g
Fats 5.6 g
Protein 9.6 g
Calories 319

4. BREAD MACHINE BASIC BREAD - EASY AS CAN BE

PREPARATION	COOKING	SERVES
5 MIN	140 MIN	1 LOAF

INGREDIENTS

- 1 cup (227 g) lukewarm water
- 1/3 cup (74 g) lukewarm milk
- Three tablespoons (43 g) butter
- 3 3/4 cups (447 g) Unbleached All-Purpose Flour

- Three tablespoons (35 g) of sugar
- 1 1/2 teaspoons salt
- 1 1/2 teaspoons of active dry yeast or instant yeast

DIRECTIONS

1. Load all the ingredients into your machine according to the manufacturer's prescribed order.
2. Program the simple white bread machine, and then press start.
3. Remove the pan from the oven when a loaf is finished. Shake the pan gently after about 5 minutes to dislodge the loaf, then turn it onto a rack to cool down.
4. Store well-wrapped, four days at the shelf, or freeze for up to 3 months.

NUTRITION

Carbohydrates 3 g
Fats 5.6 g
Protein 9.6 g
Calories 319

5. BREAD MACHINE OLIVE OIL BREAD

PREPARATION	COOKING	SERVES
15 MIN	3 HOURS	8

INGREDIENTS

- 1 cup of hot water
- 2 cups of white sugar
- 1.25 ounce of bread machine yeast
- 1/4 cup of olive oil

- 2 1/2 cups of bread flour
- 1/2 cup of whole wheat flour
- 1/2 tbsp. of salt

DIRECTIONS

1. Place the water, sugar, and leaven in the bread machine bowl. Let sit for 10 minutes — melt the yeast, and foam it.
2. Apply the oil, flour, and salt to the pot. Do not combine.
3. Set the bread machine to the configuration of white bread, and start the machine. (This takes about three hours to bake.)
4. Gobble up!

NUTRITION

Carbohydrates 3 g
Fats 5.6 g
Protein 9.6 g
Calories 319

6. HOMEMADE WHITE BREAD LESS DENSE

PREPARATION	COOKING	SERVES
10 MIN	195 MIN	8

INGREDIENTS

- 1 cup and three tablespoons of water
- Two tablespoons of vegetable oil
- 1 1/2 teaspoons of salt
- Two teaspoons of sugar
- 3 cups of white bread flour
- Two teaspoons of active dry yeast

DIRECTIONS

1. In the bread-pan, add water and oil. Stir in water, and add sugar. Add flour to a pan.
2. Create a slight indentation on top of the flour and make sure that the ingredients do not contact the flour. To the indentation, apply the yeast.
3. Keep leaven off the water.
4. Put the pan in the bread machine and press to snap it down. Secure the cover.
5. Choose the settings of 1.5 lb. loaf, basic bread, and medium crust (3 hrs. 15 minutes)
6. When the bread is baked, remove the bread pan using oven mitts. Turning over the bread pan and shaking it to release the loaf. Let the loaf reach room temperature on a wire rack for about 30 minutes.

NUTRITION

Carbohydrates 3 g
Fats 5.6 g
Protein 9.6 g
Calories 319

7. BREAD MACHINE SANDWICH BREAD

PREPARATION	COOKING	SERVES
5 MIN	25 MIN	8

INGREDIENTS

- 1 cup of heated water (45 degrees C)
- Two tablespoons of white sugar
- 2 1/4 teaspoon yeast
- 1/4 cup of olive oil
- 3 cups of bread flour
- 1 1/2 teaspoon salt

DIRECTIONS

1. Put the water, sugar, and yeast altogether in the bread machine pan.
2. Dissolve the yeast, then foam for 10 minutes.
3. Add the yeast to sugar, flour, and salt.
4. Select Basic configuration, and then press start. The entire cycle takes 3 hours to complete.

NUTRITION

Carbohydrates 3 g
Fats 5.6 g
Protein 9.6 g
Calories 319

8. BREAD MACHINE PEASANT BREAD

PREPARATION	COOKING	SERVES
20-25 MIN	25 MIN	1 LOAF

INGREDIENTS

- Two tablespoons of yeast
- 2 cups of white bread flour
- 1 1/2 tablespoon of sugar
- One tablespoon of salt
- 7/8 cup of water
- Topping of olive oil poppy seeds, sesame seeds, or cornmeal

DIRECTIONS

1. Mix yeast, flour, sugar, salt, and water in the bread machine in the manufacturer's suggested order.
2. Pick a normal setting of the bread and the light crust.
3. Upon completing the baking process, let the bread cool for 5 minutes and then remove it from the oven. Keep the bread on a cooling rack and brush lightly with olive oil on top of the loaf,
4. And sprinkle with poppy seeds, sesame seeds, or cornmeal. Before slicing or storing, let cool completely.
5. Place at room temperature in an enclosed container, or freeze.

NUTRITION

Carbohydrates 3 g
Fats 5.6 g
Protein 9.6 g
Calories 319

9. BREAD MACHINE COUNTRY WHITE BREAD

PREPARATION	COOKING	SERVES
10 MIN	120 MIN	8

INGREDIENTS

- 1 1/2 cups of water, lukewarm
- 2 1/2 cups of all-purpose flour
- 1 cup of bread flour
- 1/4 teaspoon of baking soda
- 2 1/2 teaspoons of a bread machine or instant yeast
- One tablespoon plus one teaspoon of olive oil
- 1 1/2 teaspoon of sugar
- One teaspoon of salt

DIRECTIONS

1. In the sequence suggested by your bread machine company, add all the ingredients to your bread machine pan.
2. Use the medium crust and the quick or moderate setting; press start.
3. Turn the bread out to cool onto a shelf.
4. Cut, and have fun!

NUTRITION

Carbohydrates 3 g
Fats 5.6 g
Protein 9.6 g
Calories 319

10. BEST-EVER WHEAT SANDWICH BREAD

PREPARATION	COOKING	SERVES
120 MIN	60 MIN	6

INGREDIENTS

- 1-1/3 cups plus two tbsp. of light buttermilk
- Two tbsp. of dry milk
- Three tbsp. of local honey
- Two tbsp. of extra virgin olive oil
- 1-3/4 tbsp. of white whole wheat flour
- 2-1/4 cups of bread flour
- 2 tsp. of bread machine yeast

DIRECTIONS

1. Put all the ingredients into the bread machine in the given sequence.
2. When you use the delay timer and don't make the bread right away, putting the yeast in a little well in the flour is especially important because it doesn't come into contact with any of the liquid below.
3. The process according to instructions from the manufacturer.

NUTRITION

Carbohydrates 3 g
Fats 5.6 g
Protein 9.6 g
Calories 319

11. ALMOND FLOUR BREAD

PREPARATION	COOKING	SERVES
10 MIN	10 MIN	10

INGREDIENTS

- Four egg whites
- Two egg yolks
- 2 cups almond flour
- 1/4 cup butter, melted
- 2 tbsp. psyllium husk powder
- 1 1/2 tbsp. baking powder
- 1/2 tsp. xanthan gum
- Salt
- 1/2 cup + 2 tbsp. warm water
- 2 1/4 tsp. yeast

DIRECTIONS

1. Make use of a small mixing bowl to combine the dry ingredients except for the yeast.
2. In the bread machine pan, add all the wet ingredients.
3. Add all of your dry ingredients from the lower mixing bowl to the bread machine pan. Top with the yeast.
4. Set the bread machine to the basic bread setting.
5. When the bread is completed, remove the bread machine pan from the bread machine.
6. Let cool a little before moving to a cooling rack.
7. The bread can be stored for up to 4 days on the counter and three months in the freezer.

NUTRITION

Calories: 110
Carbohydrates: 2.4g
Protein: 4g
Fat: 10g

12. COCONUT FLOUR BREAD

PREPARATION	COOKING	SERVES
10 MIN	15 MIN	12

INGREDIENTS

- Six eggs
- 1/2 cup coconut flour
- 2 tbsp. psyllium husk
- 1/4 cup olive oil
- 1 1/2 tsp. salt
- 1 tbsp. xanthan gum
- 1 tbsp. baking powder
- 2 1/4 tsp. yeast

DIRECTIONS

1. Use a small mixing bowl to combine dry ingredients except for the yeast.
2. In the bread machine pan, add all the wet ingredients.
3. Add all of your dry ingredients from the small mixing bowl to the bread machine pan. Top with the yeast.
4. Set the bread machine to the basic bread setting.
5. When the bread is done, eradicate the bread machine pan from the bread machine.
6. Let cool slightly before transferring to a cooling rack.
7. The bread can be stockpiled for up to 4 days on the counter and three months in the freezer.

NUTRITION

Calories: 174
Carbohydrates: 4g
Protein: 7g
Fat: 15g

13. CLOUD BREAD LOAF

PREPARATION	COOKING	SERVES
10 MIN	15 MIN	10

INGREDIENTS

- Six egg whites
- Six egg yolks
- 1/2 cup whey protein powder, unflavored
- 1/2 tsp. cream of tartar
- 6 oz. sour cream

- 1/2 tsp. baking powder
- 1/4 tsp. garlic powder
- 1/4 tsp. onion powder
- 1/4 tsp. salt

DIRECTIONS

1. Beat the egg whites, including the cream of tartar, till you have stiff peaks forming. Set aside.
2. Combine all other ingredients into another bowl and mix.
3. Fold the mixtures together, a little at a time.
4. Pour mixture into your bread machine pan.
5. Set the bread machine to quick bread.
6. When the bread is finished, remove the bread machine pan from the bread machine.
7. Let cool slightly before transferring to a cooling bracket.
8. The bread may be kept for up to 3 days on the counter.

NUTRITION

Calories: 90
Carbohydrates: 2g
Protein: 6g
Fat: 7g

14. SANDWICH BUNS

PREPARATION	COOKING	SERVES
10 MIN	25 MIN	8

INGREDIENTS

- Four eggs
- 2 ½ oz. almond flour
- 1 Tbsp. coconut flour
- 1 oz. psyllium
- 1 ½ cups eggplant, finely grated, juices drained
- 3 Tbsp. sesame seeds
- 1 ½ tsp. baking powder
- Salt to taste

DIRECTIONS

1. Whisk eggs until foamy, and then add grated eggplant.
2. In a separate bowl, mix all dry ingredients.
3. Add them to the egg mixture. Mix well.
4. Line a baking sheet with parchment paper, then shape the buns with your hands.
5. Bake at 374F for 20 to 25 minutes.

NUTRITION

Calories: 99
Fat: 6g
Carb: 10g
Protein: 5.3g

15. FRENCH BREAD

PREPARATION	COOKING	SERVES
150 MIN	30 MIN	14

INGREDIENTS

- 1 1/3 cups warm water
- 1 ½ tablespoon olive oil
- 1 ½ teaspoons salt
- Two tablespoons sugar
- 4 cups all-purpose flour; or bread flour
- Two teaspoons yeast

DIRECTIONS

1. Put the warm water in your bread machine first.
2. Next, put in the olive oil, then the salt, and finally the sugar. Make sure to follow that exact order. Then put in the flour. Make sure to cover the liquid ingredients.
3. In the center of the flour, make a small indentation. Make sure the indentation doesn't go down far enough to touch the liquid. Put the yeast in the indentation.
4. Set the bread machine to the French Bread Cycle.
5. After 5 minutes of kneading, check on the dough. If the dough is stiff and dry, add ½ - 1 tablespoon of water until the dough becomes a softball.
6. If the dough is too damp, add one tablespoon of flour until the right consistency is reached. Allow the bread cool for about 10 minutes, then cut it.

NUTRITION

Calories: 121
Fiber: 1.1 g
Fat: 1.9 g
Carbs: 2.9g
Protein: 3.9 g

16. GERMAN BLACK BREAD

PREPARATION	COOKING	SERVES
180 MIN	50 MIN	10

INGREDIENTS

- 1 cup water plus two tablespoons water
- Two tablespoons apple cider vinegar
- Two tablespoons molasses
- One tablespoon sugar
- One teaspoon salt
- One teaspoon instant coffee
- ¼ teaspoon fennel seeds
- One tablespoon caraway seed
- ½ ounce unsweetened chocolate
- ½ cup bran cereal flakes
- ½ cup bread flour
- ½ cup rye flour
- 2 cups whole almond flour
- One package active dry yeast

DIRECTIONS

1. Put all of the bread ingredients in your bread machine in the order listed above.
2. Start with the water and finishing with the yeast.
3. Set the bread machine to the whole wheat function.
4. Check on the dough after about 5 minutes and make sure that it's a softball.
5. Increase water one tablespoon at a time if it's too dry, and add flour one tablespoon if it's too wet.
6. When the bread is done, allow it cool on a wire rack.

NUTRITION

Calories: 102
Carbs: 3.8 g
Fiber: 3.4 g
Fat: 1.4 g
Protein: 5.0 g

17. HAZELNUT HONEY BREAD

PREPARATION	COOKING	SERVES
180 MIN	30 MIN	10

INGREDIENTS

- ½ cup lukewarm milk
- Two teaspoons butter, melted and cooled
- Two teaspoons liquid honey
- 2/3 teaspoons salt
- 1/3 cup cooked wild rice, cooled
- 1/3 cup whole grain flour
- 2/3 teaspoons caraway seeds
- 1 cup almond flour, sifted
- One teaspoon active dry yeast
- 1/3 cup hazelnuts, chopped

DIRECTIONS

1. Prepare all of the ingredients for your bread and measuring means (a cup, a spoon, kitchen scales).
2. Carefully measure the Ingredients into the pan, except the nuts and seeds.
3. Place all of the ingredients into the bread bucket in the right order.
4. Then follow the manual for your bread machine.
5. Close the cover.
6. Select the program of your bread machine to basic and choose the crust color to medium.
7. Press starts.
8. After the signal, add the nuts and seeds into the dough.
9. Wait until the program completes.
10. When done, take the bucket out and let it cool for 5-10 minutes.
11. Shake the loaf from the pan and let cool for 30 minutes on a cooling rack.
12. Slice, serve and enjoy the taste of fragrant homemade bread.

NUTRITION

Carbohydrates 5 g
Fats 2.8 g
Protein 3.6 g
Calories 113

18. BREAD WITH BEEF

PREPARATION	COOKING	SERVES
120 MIN	80 MIN	6

INGREDIENTS

- 5 oz. beef
- 15 oz. almond flour
- 5 oz. rye flour
- One onion
- Three teaspoons dry yeast

- Five tablespoons olive oil
- One tablespoon sugar
- Sea salt
- Ground black pepper

DIRECTIONS

1. Pour the warm water into the 15 oz. of the wheat flour and rye flour and leave overnight.
2. Chop the onions and cut the beef into cubes.
3. Fry the onions until transparent and golden brown and then mix in the bacon and fry on low heat for 20 minutes until soft.
4. Combine the yeast with the warm water, mixing until smooth consistency, and then combine the yeast with the flour, salt and sugar, but don't forget to mix and knead well.
5. Add in the fried onions with the beef and black pepper and mix well.
6. Pour some oil into a bread machine and place the dough into the bread maker. Shelter the dough with the towel and leave for 1 hour.
7. Close the lid and turn the bread machine on the basic/white bread program.
8. Bake the bread until after the bread is fixed, take it out, and leave for 1 hour covered with the clean, and only then can you slice the bread.

NUTRITION

Carbohydrates 6 g
Fats 21 g,
Protein 13 g
Calories 299

19. EGG BREAD

PREPARATION	COOKING	SERVES
180 MIN	30 MIN	8

INGREDIENTS

- 4 cups almond flour
- 1 cup milk
- Two eggs
- One teaspoon yeast
- 1 ½ teaspoons salt
- Two ¼ tablespoons sugar
- 1 ½ tablespoons butter

DIRECTIONS

1. Lay the products in the bread pan according to the instructions for your device. In the beginning, liquid, therefore, we pour warm milk, and we will add salt.
2. Then increase the eggs (pre-loosen with a fork) and melted butter, which must be cooled to a warm state.
3. Now add the sifted almond flour.
4. Top the yeast – dry active ones since they do not need pre-activation with liquid.
5. In the end, mix the yeast with sugar.
6. Select the basic program (on mine, it is 1 of 12). The time will automatically be set for 3 hours. When the batch begins, this is the most crucial moment. Kneading on this program lasts precisely 10 minutes, from which a ball of all products is produced.
7. Ideally, it is formed after the first 4-5 minutes of kneading; then, you can help the bread maker. First, scrape off the flour from the walls, which the blade sometimes does not entirely grasp and thus interferes with the dough. Second, you need to look carefully, as different flours from different manufacturers have different degrees of humidity, so that it may take a little more – about 2-3 tablespoons. It is when you see that the dough cannot condense and gather in a ball.
8. It is rarely rare, but sometimes there is not enough liquid, and the dough turns into lumps. If so, add a little more water and thereby help the bread maker knead the dough.
9. After exactly 3 hours, you will hear the signal, but much sooner, your home will be filled with the fantastic aroma of homemade bread. Turn off the appliance, open the lid, and take out the bowl of bread. Handsome!
10. Take out the hot egg bread and remove the paddle if it does not stay in the bowl but is at the loaf's bottom. Cool the loaves on a grate. In general, it is always advised to cool the bread on its side.
11. This bread is quite tall – 12 cm.
12. Only when the loaf completely cools you can cut the egg bread!
13. Help yourself!

NUTRITION

Carbohydrates 3 g
Fats 5.6 g
Protein 9.6 g
Calories 319

WHOLE WHEAT BREAD

20. WHOLE WHEAT BREAD

PREPARATION	COOKING	SERVES
9 MIN	4 HOURS	12 SLICES

INGREDIENTS

- Lukewarm water
- Olive oil
- Whole wheat flour sifted
- Salt
- Soft brown sugar
- Dried milk powder, skimmed
- Fast-acting, easy-blend dried yeast

DIRECTIONS

1. Add the water and olive oil to your machine, followed by half of the flour.
2. Now apply the salt, sugar, dried milk powder, and remaining flour.
3. Make a little well or dip at the top of the flour. Then carefully place the yeast into it, making sure it doesn't come into contact with any liquid.
4. Set the whole meal or whole-wheat setting according to your machine's manual, and alter the crust setting to your particular liking.
5. Once baked, carefully remove the bowl from the machine and remove the loaf, placing it on a wire rack to cool. I prefer not to add any toppings to this particular loaf, but you can, of course, experiment and add whatever you want.
6. Once cool, remove the paddle; and, for the very best results, slice with a serrated bread knife. Enjoy!

NUTRITION

Calories: 160
Carbs: 30.1g
Fat: 3,1g
Protein: 5g

21. HONEY WHOLE-WHEAT BREAD

PREPARATION	COOKING	SERVES
10 MIN	220 MIN	8 SLICES

INGREDIENTS

- Water at 90°F-100°F (320C-370C)
- Honey
- Melted butter, at room temperature
- Salt
- Whole-wheat flour
- Active dry yeast

DIRECTIONS

1. Place the ingredients in your bread machine follow the order of your manufacturer's suggestion.
2. Choose the Whole Wheat program, light or medium crust, and press START.
3. Once baked, let the loaf cool for 10 minutes.
4. Gently wiggle the bucket to remove the loaf. Then transfer it onto a rack to cool.
5. Enjoy!

NUTRITION

Calories: 101
Carbs: 19g
Fat: 2g
Protein: 4g

22. WHOLE WHEAT PEANUT BUTTER AND JELLY BREAD

PREPARATION	COOKING	SERVES
10 MIN	180 MIN	12 SLICES

INGREDIENTS

- Water at 90°F-100°F (320C-370C)
- Smooth peanut butter
- Strawberry jelly (or any preferable jelly)
- Vital wheat gluten
- Salt
- Baking soda
- Active dry yeast
- Baking powder
- Light brown sugar
- Whole wheat flour

DIRECTIONS

1. As you prep the bread machine pan, add the following in this particular order: water, jelly, salt, peanut butter, brown sugar, baking powder, baking soda, gluten, whole wheat flour, and yeast.
2. Choose 1 ½ Pound Loaf, Medium Crust, Wheat cycle, and then START the machine.
3. Once baked, place it on a rack to cool and then serve.
4. Enjoy!

NUTRITION

Calories: 230
Carbs: 39g
Fat: 6g
Protein: 9g

23. BREAD MACHINE EZEKIEL BREAD

PREPARATION	COOKING	SERVES
10 MIN	180 MIN	12 SLICES

INGREDIENTS

- Whole wheat flour
- Bread flour
- Spelled flour
- Honey
- Millet
- Olive oil
- Wheat germ

- Dry kidney beans
- Barley
- Dry lentils
- Bread machine yeast
- Dry black beans
- Water at 90°F (32OC)
- Salt

DIRECTIONS

1. Soak all beans and grains in separate bowls overnight.
2. Boil the black beans, dry kidney beans for about 1 hour, and then add lentils, millet, and barley. Next, boil for 15 minutes more.
3. Assemble boiled ingredients in a food processor and mix until mashed.
4. Spread water into the bread machine pan, add 2 tbsp. of olive oil and honey, and then add the flour, wheat germ. In one corner, add salt in another one yeast and START the Dough cycle.
5. When the bread machine beeps, add the mash to the dough and press the Whole Wheat cycle. Enjoy!

NUTRITION

Calories: 192
Carbs: 31g
Fat: 5g
Protein: 6g

24. HONEY-OAT-WHEAT BREAD

PREPARATION	COOKING	SERVES
10 MIN	3 HOURS AND 45 MIN	16 SLICES

INGREDIENTS

- Active dry yeast
- Sugar
- Water at 1100F (450C)
- All-purpose flour
- Whole wheat flour
- Rolled oats
- Powdered milk
- Salt
- Honey
- Vegetable oil
- Butter softened
- Cooking spray

DIRECTIONS

1. Place the following into the pan of a bread machine: yeast, sugar, and water. Let the yeast dissolve and foam for approximately 10 minutes. In the meantime, in a bowl, combine the all-purpose flour, powdered milk, whole wheat flour, salt, and rolled oats. Pour the butter, honey, and vegetable oil into the yeast mixture. Then add the flour mixture on top.
2. Choose the Dough cycle and then push the START button. Let the bread machine fully finish the process, which spans approximately 1 ½ hour. Place the dough into a 9x5-inch loaf pan that's coated with cooking spray. Leave the bread to rise in a warm place for 1 hour.
3. Preheat the oven.
4. Bake for approximately 35 minutes in the warmed oven until the top turns golden brown.
5. Enjoy!

NUTRITION

Calories: 281
Carbs: 45g
Fat: 9g
Protein: 6g

25. BUTTER UP BREAD

PREPARATION	COOKING	SERVES
10 MIN	180 MIN	12 SLICES

INGREDIENTS

- Bread flour
- Margarine, melted
- Buttermilk at 1100F (450C)
- Sugar

- Active dry yeast
- Egg, at room temperature
- Salt

DIRECTIONS

1. Prepare the bread machine pan by adding buttermilk, melted margarine, salt, sugar, flour, and yeast in the order specified by your manufacturer.
2. Select Basic/White Setting and press START.
3. Once baked, transfer onto wire racks to cool before slicing.
4. Enjoy!

NUTRITION

Calories: 231
Carbs: 36g
Fat: 6g
Protein: 8g

26. BUTTER HONEY WHEAT BREAD

PREPARATION	COOKING	SERVES
5 MIN	3 HOURS AND 45 MIN	12 SLICES

INGREDIENTS

- Buttermilk
- Butter, melted
- Honey
- Bread flour
- Whole wheat flour
- Salt
- Baking soda
- Active dry yeast

DIRECTIONS

1. Put all ingredients into the bread machine, by way of recommended by the manufacturer.
2. In my case, liquids always go first.
3. Run the bread machine for a loaf (1½ lbs.) on the Whole Wheat setting.
4. Once the baking process is done, transfer the baked bread to a wire rack and cool before slicing.
5. Enjoy!

NUTRITION

Calories: 170
Carbs: 27g
Fat: 6g
Protein: 3g

27. BUTTERMILK WHEAT BREAD

PREPARATION	COOKING	SERVES
8 MIN	4 HOURS AND 30 MIN	16 SLICES

INGREDIENTS

- Buttermilk, at room temperature
- White sugar
- Olive oil
- Salt
- Baking soda
- Unbleached white flour
- Whole wheat flour
- Active dry yeast

DIRECTIONS

1. In the bread machine pan, measure all ingredients in the order the manufacturer recommends.
2. Set the machine to the Basic White Bread setting and press START.
3. After a few minutes, add more buttermilk if the ingredients don't form a ball. If it's too loose, apply a handful of flour.
4. One baked, let the bread cool on a wire rack before slicing.
5. Enjoy!

NUTRITION

Calories: 141
Carbs: 26g
Fat: 2.5g
Protein: 5g

28. CRACKED FIT AND FAT BREAD

PREPARATION	COOKING	SERVES
5 MIN	3 HOURS AND 25 MIN	16 SLICES

INGREDIENTS

- Water
- Butter softened
- Brown sugar
- Salt

- Bread flour
- Whole wheat flour
- Cracked wheat
- Active dry yeast

DIRECTIONS

1. In the bread machine pan, measure all components according to the manufacturer's suggested order.
2. Choose Basic/White cycle, medium crust, and 2lbs weight of loaf, and then press START.
3. Once baked, allow the bread to cool on a wire rack before slicing.
4. Enjoy!

NUTRITION

Calories: 65
Carbs: 12.4g
Fat: 1g
Protein: 2g

29. CRUNCHY HONEY WHEAT BREAD

PREPARATION	COOKING	SERVES
7 MIN	3 HOURS AND 30 MIN	12 SLICES

INGREDIENTS

- Warm water at 110OF (45OC)
- Vegetable oil
- Honey
- Salt

- Bread flour
- Whole wheat flour
- Granola
- Active dry yeast

DIRECTIONS

1. Place the ingredients into the bread machine following the order recommended by the manufacturer.
2. Choose the Whole Wheat setting or the Dough cycle on the machine. Press the START button.
3. Once the machine has finished the whole cycle of baking the bread in the oven, form the dough and add it into a loaf pan that's greased. Let it rise in volume in a warm place until it becomes double its size. Insert into the preheated 350°F (175°C) oven and bake for 35-45 minutes.
4. Enjoy!

NUTRITION

Calories: 199
Carbs: 37g
Fat: 4.2g
Protein: 6.2g

30. EASY HOME BASE WHEAT BREAD

PREPARATION	COOKING	SERVES
10 MIN	3 HOURS AND 50 MIN	12 SLICES

INGREDIENTS

- Whole wheat flour
- Bread flour
- Butter softened
- Warm water at 900F (320C)
- Warm milk at 900F (320C)

- Active dry yeast
- Egg, at room temperature
- Salt
- Honey

DIRECTIONS

1. Add the ingredients into the pan of the bread machine following the order suggested by the manufacturer.
2. Use the Whole Wheat cycle, choose the crust color, weight, and START the machine.
3. Check how the dough is kneading after five minutes pass because you may need to add either one tbsp. of water or one tbsp. of flour-based on consistency.
4. When the bread is complete, cool it on a wire rack before slicing.
5. Enjoy!

NUTRITION

Calories: 180
Carbs: 33g
Fat: 2g
Protein: 7g

31. WHOLE WHEAT YOGURT BREAD

PREPARATION	COOKING	SERVES
10 MIN	3 HOURS AND 40 MIN	12 SLICES

INGREDIENTS

- Ground nutmeg (optional)
- Water
- Butter, melted
- Plain yogurt
- Dry milk
- Honey
- Active dry yeast
- Whole wheat flour
- Bread flour
- Ground cinnamon
- Salt

DIRECTIONS

1. Begin by pouring ingredients into the bread pan in the instruction your manufacturer endorses. In my case, liquids always go first.
2. So, I begin with water, yogurt, butter, honey, sieve flour, dry milk, add salt, ground cinnamon, and yeast in different corners of the pan.
3. Select the Whole grain setting, light or medium crust, and press START.
4. When ready, allow it to cool and then serve.
5. Enjoy!

NUTRITION

Calories: 158
Carbs: 20g
Fat: 5g
Protein: 6g

GRAIN SEED & NUT BREAD

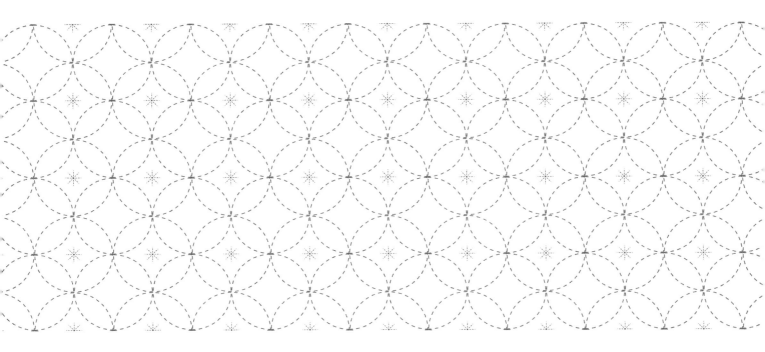

32. NUTRITIOUS 9-GRAIN BREAD

PREPARATION	COOKING	SERVES	DIFFICULTY
5 MIN	120 MIN	10 SLICES	BEGINNERS

INGREDIENTS

- Warm water – 3/4 cup+2 tablespoons.
- Whole wheat flour – 1 cup.
- Bread flour – 1 cup.
- 9-grain cereal – ½ cup., crushed
- Salt – 1 teaspoon.
- Butter – 1 tablespoon.
- Sugar – 2 tablespoons.
- Milk powder – 1 tablespoon.
- Active dry yeast – 2 teaspoons.

NUTRITION

Calories 132,
Carbs 25g,
Fat 1.7g,
Protein 4.1g

DIRECTIONS

1. Put all ingredients into the bread machine.
2. Select whole wheat setting then select light/medium crust and start.
3. Once loaf is done, remove the loaf pan from the machine.
4. Allow it to cool for 10 minutes. Slice and serve.

33. OATMEAL SUNFLOWER BREAD

PREPARATION	COOKING	SERVES	DIFFICULTY
15 MIN	3 HOURS AND 30 MIN	10 SLICES	BEGINNERS

INGREDIENTS

- Water – 1 cup.
- Honey – ¼ cup.
- Butter – 2 tablespoons., softened
- Bread flour – 3 cups.
- Old fashioned oats – ½ cup.

- Milk powder – 2 tablespoons.
- Salt – 1 ¼ teaspoons.
- Active dry yeast – 2 ¼ teaspoons.
- Sunflower seeds – ½ cup.

NUTRITION

Calories 215,
Carbs 39.3g,
Fat 4.2g,
Protein 5.4g

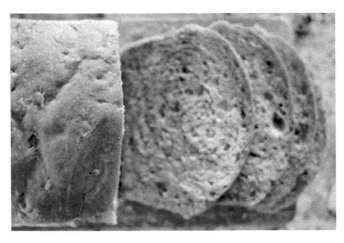

DIRECTIONS

1. Add all ingredients except for sunflower seeds into the bread machine pan.
2. Select basic setting then select light/medium crust and press start. Add sunflower seeds just before the final kneading cycle.
3. Once loaf is done, remove the loaf pan from the machine. Allow it to cool for 10 minutes. Slice and serve.

34. CORNMEAL WHOLE WHEAT BREAD

PREPARATION	COOKING	SERVES	DIFFICULTY
10 MIN	120 MIN	10 SLICES	BEGINNERS

INGREDIENTS

- Active dry yeast – 2 ½ teaspoons.
- Water – 1 1/3 cups.
- Sugar – 2 tablespoons.
- Egg – 1, lightly beaten
- Butter – 2 tablespoons.
- Salt – 1 ½ teaspoons.
- Cornmeal – 3/4 cup.
- Whole wheat flour – 3/4 cup.
- Bread flour – 2 3/4 cups.

NUTRITION

Calories 228,
Carbs 41.2g,
Fat 3.3g,
Protein 7.1g

DIRECTIONS

1. Add all ingredients to the bread machine pan according to the bread machine manufacturer instructions.
2. Select basic bread setting then select medium crust and start. Once loaf is done, remove the loaf pan from the machine.
3. Allow it to cool for 10 minutes. Slice and serve.

35. DELICIOUS CRANBERRY BREAD

PREPARATION	COOKING	SERVES	DIFFICULTY
5 MIN	3 HOURS AND 27 MIN	10 SLICES	BEGINNERS

INGREDIENTS

- Warm water – 1 ½ cups
- Brown sugar – 2 tablespoons.
- Salt – 1 ½ teaspoons.
- Olive oil – 2 tablespoons.
- Flour – 4 cups

- Cinnamon – 1 ½ teaspoons.
- Cardamom – 1 ½ teaspoons.
- Dried cranberries – 1 cup
- Yeast – 2 teaspoons

NUTRITION

Calories 223,
Carbs 41.9g,
Fat 3.3g,
Protein 5.5g

DIRECTIONS

1. Put all ingredients to the bread machine in the listed order.
2. Select sweet bread setting then select light/medium crust and start. Once loaf is done, remove the loaf pan from the machine.
3. Allow it to cool for 20 minutes. Slice and serve.

36. COFFEE RAISIN BREAD

PREPARATION	COOKING	SERVES	DIFFICULTY
15 MIN	3 HOURS	10 SLICES	BEGINNERS

INGREDIENTS

- Active dry yeast — 2 ½ teaspoons.
- Ground cloves — ¼ teaspoon.
- Ground allspice — ¼ teaspoon.
- Ground cinnamon — 1 teaspoon.
- Sugar — 3 tablespoons.
- Egg — 1, lightly beaten

- Olive oil — 3 tablespoons.
- Strong brewed coffee — 1 cup.
- Bread flour — 3 cups.
- Raisins — 3/4 cup.
- Salt — 1 ½ teaspoons

NUTRITION

Calories 230,
Carbs 41.5g,
Fat 5.1g,
Protein 5.2g

DIRECTIONS

1. Add all ingredients except for raisins into the bread machine pan.
2. Select basic setting then select light/medium crust and press start. Add raisins just before the final kneading cycle.
3. Once loaf is done, remove the loaf pan from the machine. Allow it to cool for 10 minutes. Slice and serve.

37. HEALTHY MULTIGRAIN BREAD

PREPARATION	COOKING	SERVES	DIFFICULTY
5 MIN	40 MIN	10 SLICES	BEGINNERS

INGREDIENTS

- Water – 1 ¼ cups.
- Butter – 2 tablespoons.
- Bread flour – 1 1/3 cups.
- Whole wheat flour – 1 ½ cups.
- Multigrain cereal – 1 cup.
- Brown sugar – 3 tablespoons.
- Salt – 1 ¼ teaspoons.
- Yeast – 2 ½ teaspoons

NUTRITION

Calories 159,
Carbs 29.3g,
Fat 2.9g,
Protein 4.6g

DIRECTIONS

1. Put ingredients listed into the bread machine pan. Select basic bread setting then select light/medium crust and start.
2. Once loaf is done, remove the loaf pan from the machine. Allow it to cool for 10 minutes. Slice and serve.

38. ITALIAN PINE NUT BREAD

PREPARATION	COOKING	SERVES	DIFFICULTY
5 MIN	3 HOURS AND 30 MIN	10 SLICES	BEGINNERS

INGREDIENTS

- Water – 1 cup+ 2 tablespoons.
- Bread flour – 3 cups.
- Sugar – 2 tablespoons.
- Salt – 1 teaspoon.
- Active dry yeast – 1 1/4 teaspoons.
- Basil pesto – 1/3 cup.
- Flour – 2 tablespoons.
- Pine nuts – 1/3 cup

NUTRITION

Calories 180,
Carbs 32.4g,
Fat 3.5g,
Protein 4.8g

DIRECTIONS

1. In a small container, combine basil pesto and flour and mix until well blended. Add pine nuts and stir well. Add water, bread flour, sugar, salt, and yeast into the bread machine pan.
2. Select basic setting then select medium crust and press start. Add basil pesto mixture just before the final kneading cycle.
3. Once loaf is done, remove the loaf pan from the machine. Allow it to cool for 10 minutes. Slice and serve.

39. WHOLE WHEAT RAISIN BREAD

PREPARATION	COOKING	SERVES	DIFFICULTY
5 MIN	120 MIN	10 SLICES	BEGINNERS

INGREDIENTS

- Whole wheat flour — 3 ½ cups
- Dry yeast — 2 teaspoons.
- Eggs — 2, lightly beaten
- Butter — ¼ cup, softened
- Water — 3/4 cup
- Milk — 1/3 cup
- Salt — 1 teaspoon.

- Sugar — 1/3 cup
- Cinnamon — 4 teaspoons.
- Raisins — 1 cup

NUTRITION

Calories 290,
Carbs 53.1g,
Fat 6.2g,
Protein 6.8g

DIRECTIONS

1. Add water, milk, butter, and eggs to the bread pan. Add remaining ingredients except for yeast to the bread pan.
2. Make a small hole into the flour with your finger and add yeast to the hole. Make sure yeast will not be mixed with any liquids.
3. Select whole wheat setting then select light/medium crust and start. Once loaf is done, remove the loaf pan from the machine.
4. Allow it to cool for 10 minutes. Slice and serve.

40. HEALTHY SPELT BREAD

PREPARATION	COOKING	SERVES	DIFFICULTY
15 MIN	40 MIN	10 SLICES	BEGINNERS

INGREDIENTS

- Milk – 1 ¼ cups.
- Sugar – 2 tablespoons.
- Olive oil – 2 tablespoons.
- Salt – 1 teaspoon.
- Spelt flour – 4 cups.
- Yeast – 2 ½ teaspoons

NUTRITION

Calories 223,
Carbs 40.3g,
Fat 4.5g,
Protein 9.2g

DIRECTIONS

1. Add all ingredients according to the bread machine manufacturer instructions into the bread machine.
2. Select basic bread setting then select light/medium crust and start. Once loaf is done, remove the loaf pan from the machine.
3. Allow it to cool for 10 minutes. Slice and serve.

41. AWESOME ROSEMARY BREAD

PREPARATION	COOKING	SERVES	DIFFICULTY
5 MIN	120 MIN	8 SLICES	BEGINNERS

INGREDIENTS

- 3/4 cup + 1 tablespoon water at 80 degrees F
- 1 2/3 tablespoons melted butter, cooled
- 2 teaspoons sugar
- 1 teaspoon salt
- 1 tablespoon fresh rosemary, chopped
- 2 cups white bread flour
- 1 1/3 teaspoons instant yeast

NUTRITION

Total Carbs: 25g
Fiber: 1g
Protein: 4g
Fat: 3g
Calories: 142

DIRECTIONS

1. Combine all of the ingredients to your bread machine, carefully following the instructions of the manufacturer.
2. Set the program of your bread machine to Basic/White Bread and set crust type to Medium.
3. Press START.
4. Wait until the cycle completes.
5. Once the loaf is ready, take the bucket out and allow the loaf to chill for 5 minutes.
6. Gently jiggle the bucket to take out the loaf.

42. FLAX AND SUNFLOWER SEED BREAD

PREPARATION	COOKING	SERVES
5 MIN	25 MIN	8

INGREDIENTS

- 1 1/3 cups water
- Two tablespoons butter softened
- Three tablespoons honey
- 2/3 cups of bread flour
- One teaspoon salt
- One teaspoon active dry yeast
- 1/2 cup flax seeds
- 1/2 cup sunflower seeds

DIRECTIONS

1. With the manufacturer's suggested order, add all the ingredients (apart from sunflower seeds) to the bread machine's pan.
2. The select basic white cycle, then press start.
3. Just in the knead cycle that your machine signals alert sounds, add the sunflower seeds.

NUTRITION

Calories: 140 calories;　　Cholesterol: 4
Sodium: 169　　　　　　　Protein: 4.2
Total Carbohydrate: 22.7　Total Fat: 4.2

43. HONEY AND FLAXSEED BREAD

PREPARATION	COOKING	SERVES
5 MIN	25 MIN	8

INGREDIENTS

- 1 1/8 cups water
- 1 1/2 tablespoons flaxseed oil
- Three tablespoons honey
- 1/2 tablespoon liquid lecithin
- cups whole wheat flour
- 1/2 cup flax seed
- Two tablespoons bread flour
- Three tablespoons whey powder
- 1 1/2 teaspoons sea salt
- Two teaspoons active dry yeast

DIRECTIONS

1. In the bread machine pan, put in all of the ingredients following the order recommended by the manufacturer.
2. Choose the Wheat cycle on the machine and press the Start button to run the machine.

NUTRITION

Calories: 174 calories;
Protein: 7.1
Total Fat: 4.9

Sodium: 242
Total Carbohydrate: 30.8
Cholesterol: 1

44. PUMPKIN AND SUNFLOWER SEED BREAD

PREPARATION	COOKING	SERVES
5 MIN	25 MIN	8

INGREDIENTS

- 1 (.25 ounce) package instant yeast
- 1 cup of warm water
- 1/4 cup honey
- Four teaspoons vegetable oil
- cups whole wheat flour
- 1/4 cup wheat bran (optional)
- One teaspoon salt
- 1/3 cup sunflower seeds
- 1/3 cup shelled, toasted, chopped pumpkin seeds

DIRECTIONS

1. Into the bread machine, put the ingredients according to the order suggested by the manufacturer.
2. Next is setting the machine to the whole wheat setting, then press the start button.
3. You can add the pumpkin and sunflower seeds at the beep if your bread machine has a signal for nuts or fruit.

NUTRITION

Calories: 148 calories;
Total Carbohydrate: 24.1
Cholesterol: 0
Protein: 5.1
Total Fat: 4.8
Sodium: 158

45. SEVEN GRAIN BREAD

PREPARATION	COOKING	SERVES
5 MIN	25 MIN	8

INGREDIENTS

- 1 1/3 cups warm water
- One tablespoon active dry yeast
- Three tablespoons dry milk powder
- Two tablespoons vegetable oil
- Two tablespoons honey
- Two teaspoons salt
- One egg
- 1 cup whole wheat flour
- 1/2 cups bread flour
- 3/4 cup 7-grain cereal

DIRECTIONS

1. Follow the order of putting the ingredients into the pan of the bread machine recommended by the manufacturer.
2. Choose the Whole Wheat Bread cycle on the machine and press the Start button to run the machine.

NUTRITION

Calories: 285 calories;   50.6
Total Fat: 5.2   Cholesterol: 24
Sodium: 629   Protein: 9.8
Total Carbohydrate:

46. WHEAT BREAD WITH FLAX SEED

PREPARATION	COOKING	SERVES
5 MIN	25 MIN	8

INGREDIENTS

- 1 (.25 ounce) package active dry yeast
- 1 1/4 cups whole wheat flour
- 3/4 cup ground flax seed
- 1 cup bread flour
- One tablespoon vital wheat gluten
- Two tablespoons dry milk powder
- One teaspoon salt
- 1 1/2 tablespoons vegetable oil
- 1/4 cup honey
- 1 1/2 cups water

DIRECTIONS

1. In the bread machine pan, put the ingredients following the order recommendation of the manufacturer.
2. Make sure to select the cycle and then press Start.

NUTRITION

Calories: 168 calories
Total Carbohydrate: 22.5
Cholesterol: 1

Protein: 5.5
Total Fat: 7.3
Sodium: 245

47. HIGH FIBER BREAD

PREPARATION	COOKING	SERVES
5 MIN	25 MIN	8

INGREDIENTS

- 1 2/3 cups warm water
- Four teaspoons molasses
- One tablespoon active dry yeast
- 2/3 cups whole wheat flour
- 3/4 cup ground flax seed
- 2/3 cup bread flour
- 1/2 cup oat bran
- 1/3 cup rolled oats
- 1/3 cup amaranth seeds
- One teaspoon salt

DIRECTIONS

1. In the bread machine pan, put in the water, molasses, yeast, wheat flour, ground flaxseed, bread flour, oat bran, rolled oats, amaranth seeds, and salt in the manufacturer's suggested order of ingredients. Choose the Dough cycle on the machine and press the Start button; let the machine finish the whole Dough cycle.
2. Put the dough on a clean surface that is covered with a little bit of flour. Shape the dough into two loaves and put it on a baking stone. Use a slightly wet cloth to shelter the loaves and allow it to rise in volume for about 1 hour until it has doubled in size.
3. Preheat the oven to 375°F.
4. Put in the warm-up oven and bake for 20-25 minutes until the top part of the loaf turns golden brown. Let the loaf slide onto a clean working surface and tap the loaf's bottom part gently. The bread is done if you hear a hollow sound when tapped.

NUTRITION

Calories: 101 calories;
Total Fat: 2.1
Sodium: 100

Total Carbohydrate: 18.2
Cholesterol: 0
Protein: 4

48. HIGH FLAVOR BRAN HEAD

PREPARATION	COOKING	SERVES
5 MIN	25 MIN	8

INGREDIENTS

- 1 1/2 cups warm water
- Two tablespoons dry milk powder
- Two tablespoons vegetable oil
- Two tablespoons molasses
- Two tablespoons honey
- 1 1/2 teaspoons salt
- 1/4 cups whole wheat flour
- 1 1/4 cups bread flour
- 1 cup whole bran cereal
- Two teaspoons active dry yeast

DIRECTIONS

1. In the pan of your bread machine, move all the ingredients directed by the machine's maker.
2. Set the machine to either the whole grain or whole wheat setting.

NUTRITION

Calories: 146 calories
Total Fat: 2.4
Sodium: 254

Total Carbohydrate: 27.9
Cholesterol: 1
Protein: 4.6

49. HIGH PROTEIN BREAD

PREPARATION	COOKING	SERVES
5 MIN	25 MIN	8

INGREDIENTS

- Two teaspoons active dry yeast
- 1 cup bread flour
- 1 cup whole wheat flour
- 1/4 cup soy flour
- 1/4 cup powdered soy milk
- 1/4 cup oat bran
- One tablespoon canola oil
- One tablespoon honey
- One teaspoon salt
- 1 cup of water

DIRECTIONS

1. Into the bread machine's pan, put the ingredients by following the order suggested by the manufacturer.
2. Set the machine to either the regular setting or the basic medium.
3. Push the Start button.

NUTRITION

Calories: 137 calories
Total Fat: 2.4
Sodium: 235

Total Carbohydrate: 24.1
Cholesterol: 0
Protein: 6.5

50. WHOLE WHEAT BREAD WITH SESAME SEEDS

PREPARATION	COOKING	SERVES
5 MIN	25 MIN	8

INGREDIENTS

- 1/2 cup water
- Two teaspoons honey
- One tablespoon vegetable oil
- 3/4 cup grated zucchini
- 3/4 cup whole wheat flour
- cups bread flour
- One tablespoon chopped fresh basil
- Two teaspoons sesame seeds
- One teaspoon salt
- 1 1/2 teaspoons active dry yeast

DIRECTIONS

1. Follow the order of putting the ingredients into the bread machine pan recommended by the manufacturer.
2. Choose the Basic Bread cycle or the Normal setting on the machine.

NUTRITION

Calories: 153 calories
Sodium: 235
Total Carbohydrate: 28.3
Cholesterol: 0
Protein: 5
Total Fat: 2.3

51. BAGELS WITH POPPY SEEDS

PREPARATION	COOKING	SERVES
5 MIN	25 MIN	8

INGREDIENTS

- 1 cup of warm water
- 1 1/2 teaspoons salt
- Two tablespoons white sugar
- cups bread flour
- 1/4 teaspoons active dry yeast
- quarts boiling water
- Three tablespoons white sugar
- One tablespoon cornmeal
- One egg white
- Three tablespoons poppy seeds

DIRECTIONS

1. In the bread machine's pan, pour in the water, salt, sugar, flour, and yeast following the order of ingredients suggested by the manufacturer. Choose the Dough setting on the machine.

2. Once the machine has finished the whole cycle, place the dough on a clean surface covered with a little bit of flour; let it rest. While the dough is resting on the floured surface, put 3 quarts of water in a big pot and let it boil. Add in 3 tablespoons of sugar and mix.

3. Divide the dough evenly into nine portions and shape each into a small ball. Press down each dough ball until it is flat. Use your thumb to make a shack in the center of each flattened dough. Increase the whole's size in the center and smoothen out the dough around the whole area by spinning the dough on your thumb or finger. Use a clean cloth to cover the formed bagels and let it sit for 10 minutes.

4. Cover the bottom part of an ungreased baking sheet evenly with cornmeal. Place the bagels gently into the boiling water. Let it boil for 1 minute and flip it on the other side halfway through. Let the bagels drain quickly on a clean towel. Place the boiled bagels onto the prepared baking sheet. Coat the topmost of each bagel with egg white and top it off with your preferred toppings.

5. Put the bagels into the preheated 375°F (190°C) oven and bake for 20-25 minutes until it turns nice brown.

NUTRITION

Calories: 50 calories
Total Fat: 1.3
Sodium: 404
Total Carbohydrate: 8.8

Cholesterol: 0
Protein: 1.4

52. BRUCE'S HONEY SESAME BREAD

PREPARATION	COOKING	SERVES
5 MIN	25 MIN	8

INGREDIENTS

- 1 1/4 cups water
- 1/4 cup honey
- One tablespoon powdered buttermilk
- 1 1/2 teaspoons salt
- cups bread flour
- Three tablespoons wheat bran
- 1/2 cup sesame seeds, toasted
- 1/4 teaspoons active dry yeast

DIRECTIONS

1. Into the bread machine's pan, place all the ingredients by following the order endorsed by your machine's manufacturer.
2. Set the mechanism to the Basic Bread cycle.

NUTRITION

Calories: 62 calories
Total Carbohydrate: 8.4
Cholesterol: 1

Protein: 1.7
Total Fat: 3.1
Sodium: 295

53. MOROCCAN KSRA

PREPARATION	COOKING	SERVES
5 MIN	25 MIN	8

INGREDIENTS

- 7/8 cup water
- 1/4 cups bread flour
- 3/4 cup semolina flour
- One teaspoon anise seed
- 1 1/2 teaspoons salt
- 1/2 teaspoon white sugar
- Two teaspoons active dry yeast
- One tablespoon olive oil
- One tablespoon sesame seed

DIRECTIONS

1. In a bread machine, put the first set of ingredients according to the manufacturer's recommendation. Set to DOUGH cycle and select Start. In this procedure, refrain from mixing in the sesame seeds and olive oil.
2. When the dough cycle signal stops, take the dough from the machine and deflate by punching down. Cut the dough into two halves and form it into balls. Pat the balls into a 3/4-inch thickness. Put the flattened dough on a floured baking sheet. Cover the baking sheet with towels and let it stand for about 30 minutes to rise to double.
3. Set the oven to 200 degrees C (400 degrees F) to preheat. Spread the top of the loaves with olive oil using a brush and garnish with sesame seeds, if preferred. Using a fork, puncture the top of each loaf all over.
4. Place the pans in the heated oven, then bake for 20 to 25 minutes, or until colors are golden and they sound hollow when tapped. Serve either warm or cold.

NUTRITION

Calories: 111 calories
Total Fat: 1.6
Sodium: 219
Total Carbohydrate: 20.2
Cholesterol: 0
Protein: 3.6

54. BREAD STICKS WITH SESAME SEEDS

PREPARATION	COOKING	SERVES
5 MIN	25 MIN	8

INGREDIENTS

- 1 1/3 cups warm water
- Three tablespoons butter softened
- cups bread flour
- Two teaspoons salt

- 1/4 cup white sugar
- 1/4 cup sesame seeds
- Two tablespoons dry milk powder
- 1/2 teaspoons active dry yeast

DIRECTIONS

1. Into the bread machine pan, set the ingredients according to the order given by the manufacturer. Put the machine to the Dough cycle and then push the Start button. Use cooking spray to spritz two baking sheets.

2. Preheat the oven. After the dough cycle comes to an end, place the dough onto a lightly oiled surface. Separate the dough into 18 pieces. Fold every piece on a board oiled from the middle of the amount to the outside edges. It is to create breadsticks. Transfer the breadsticks onto the prepared pans placing at least one inch apart.

3. Bake for around 15 minutes using the oven until golden. Transfer to a wire rack to cool.

NUTRITION

Calories: 154
Total Fat: 3.5
Sodium: 278

Total Carbohydrate: 26
Cholesterol: 5
Protein: 4.5

55. OAT MOLASSES BREAD

PREPARATION	COOKING	SERVES
120 MIN	60 MIN	1 LOAF

INGREDIENTS

- 16 slice bread (2 pounds)
- 1 1/3 cups boiling water
- ¾ cup old-fashioned oats
- Three tablespoons butter
- One large egg, lightly beaten
- Two teaspoons table salt
- ¼ cup honey
- 1½ tablespoons dark molasses
- 4 cups white bread flour
- 2½ teaspoons bread machine yeast

- 12 slice bread (1½ pounds)
- 1 cup boiling water
- ½ cup old-fashioned oats
- Two tablespoons butter
- One large egg, lightly beaten
- 1½ teaspoons table salt
- Three tablespoons honey
- One tablespoon dark molasses
- 3 cups white bread flour
- Two teaspoons bread machine yeast

DIRECTIONS

1. Add the boiling water and oats to a mixing bowl. Allow the oats to soak well and cool down completely. Do not drain the water.
2. Choose the size of bread you would like to make, then measure your ingredients.
3. Add the soaked oats, along with any remaining water, to the bread pan.
4. Put the remaining ingredients in the bread pan in the order listed above.
5. Place the pan in the bread machine, then cover.
6. Press on the machine. Select the Basic setting, then the loaf size, and finally, the crust color. Start the cycle.
7. When the process is finished, then when the bread is baked, remove the pan. Use a potholder as the handle. Rest for a while
8. Take out the bread from the pan and place it in a wire rack. Let it cool for at least 10 minutes before slicing.

NUTRITION

Calories 160,
Fat 7.1 g,
carbs 18 g,

sodium 164 mg,
protein 5.1 g

CHEESE BREAD

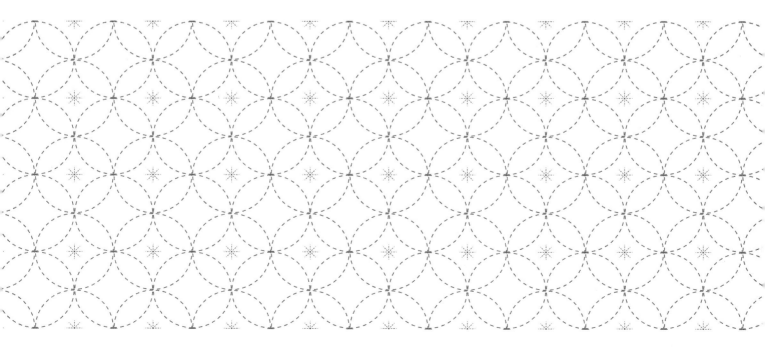

56. CHEESE BUTTERMILK BREAD

PREPARATION	COOKING	SERVES
5 MIN	120 MIN	10

INGREDIENTS

- Buttermilk – 1 1/8 cups
- Active dry yeast – 1 ½ tsp.
- Cheddar cheese – ¾ cup., shredded
- Sugar – 1 ½ tsp.
- Bread flour – 3 cups.
- Buttermilk – 1 1/8 cups.
- Salt – 1 1/2 tsp.

DIRECTIONS

1. Place all ingredients into the bread machine pan based on the bread machine manufacturer instructions.
2. Select basic bread setting, then select light/medium crust and start.
3. Once the loaf is done, remove the loaf pan from the machine.
4. Allow it to cool for 10 minutes.
5. Slice and serve.

NUTRITION

Calories 182
Carbs 30g
Fat 3.4g
Protein 6.8g

57. DELICIOUS ITALIAN CHEESE BREAD

PREPARATION	COOKING	SERVES
5 MIN	120 MIN	10

INGREDIENTS

- Active dry yeast — 2 tsp.
- Brown sugar — 2 tbsp.
- Parmesan cheese — 2 tbsp., grated
- Ground black pepper — 1 tsp.
- Italian seasoning — 2 tsp.
- Pepper jack cheese — 1/2 cup., shredded
- Bread flour — 3 cups.
- Warm water — 1 ¼ cups
- Salt — 1 ½ tsp.

DIRECTIONS

1. First, add all ingredients to the bread machine pan.
2. Select a basic setting, then select a light/medium crust and start.
3. Once the loaf is done, remove the loaf pan from the machine.
4. Allow it to cool for 10 minutes.
5. Slice and serve.

NUTRITION

Calories 163
Carbs 31.1g
Fat 1.8g
Protein 5.3g

58. BEER CHEESE BREAD

PREPARATION	COOKING	SERVES
5 MIN	120 MIN	10

INGREDIENTS

- Monterey Jack cheese – 4 oz., shredded
- American cheese – 4 oz., shredded
- Beer – 10 oz.
- Butter – 1 tbsp.
- Sugar – 1 tbsp.
- Bread flour – 3 cups.
- Active dry yeast – 1 packet
- Salt – 1 ½ tsp

DIRECTIONS

1. Place the ingredients into the pan of the bread machine.
2. Select the basic setting, then select a light crust and start.
3. Once the loaf is done, remove the loaf pan from the machine.
4. Allow it to cool for 10 minutes.
5. Slice and serve.

NUTRITION

Calories 245
Carbs 32.1g
Fat 7.8g
Protein 9.2g

59. MOIST CHEDDAR CHEESE BREAD

PREPARATION	COOKING	SERVES
5 MIN	3 HOURS AND 45 MIN	10

INGREDIENTS

- Milk – 1 cup
- Butter – ½ cup, melted
- All-purpose flour – 3 cups
- Cheddar cheese – 2 cups, shredded
- Garlic powder – ½ tsp.
- Kosher salt – 2 tsp.
- Sugar – 1 tbsp.
- Active dry yeast – 1 ¼ oz

DIRECTIONS

1. Add milk and butter into the bread pan.
2. Add remaining ingredients except for yeast to the bread pan.
3. Make a narrow hole into the flour with your finger and add yeast to the punch.
4. Make sure yeast will not be mixed with any liquids.
5. Select the basic setting, then select a light crust and start.
6. Once the loaf is done, remove the loaf pan from the machine.
7. Allow it to cool for 10 minutes.
8. Slice and serve.

NUTRITION

Calories 337
Carbs 32.8g
Fat 17.7g
Protein 11.8g

60. CHEESE PEPPERONI BREAD

PREPARATION	COOKING	SERVES
5 MIN	120 MIN	10

INGREDIENTS

- Pepperoni — 2/3 cup, diced
- Active dry yeast — 1 ½ tsp.
- Bread flour — 3 ¼ cups.
- Dried oregano — 1 ½ tsp.
- Garlic salt — 1 ½ tsp.
- Sugar — 2 tbsp.
- Mozzarella cheese — 1/3 cup., shredded
- Warm water — 1 cup+2 tbsp

DIRECTIONS

1. Add all ingredients except for pepperoni into the bread machine pan.
2. Select basic setting, then selects medium crust and press start.
3. Add pepperoni just before the final kneading cycle.
4. Once the loaf is done, remove the loaf pan from the machine.
5. Allow it to cool for 10 minutes.
6. Slice and serve.

NUTRITION

Calories 176
Carbs 34.5g
Fat 1.5g
Protein 5.7g

61. GLUTEN-FREE CHEESY BREAD

PREPARATION	COOKING	SERVES
5 MIN	4 HOURS	10

INGREDIENTS

- Eggs – 3
- Olive oil – 2 tbsp.
- Water – 1 ½ cups.
- Active dry yeast – 2 ¼ tsp.
- White rice flour – 2 cups.
- Brown rice flour – 1 cup.
- Milk powder – ¼ cup.
- Sugar – 2 tbsp.
- Poppy seeds – 1 tbsp.
- Xanthan gum – 3 ½ tsp.
- Cheddar cheese – 1 ½ cups., shredded
- Salt – 1 tsp

DIRECTIONS

1. In a bowl, mix eggs, water, and oil and pour it into the bread machine pan.
2. In a large bowl, mix the other ingredients and pour over wet ingredient mixture into the bread pan.
3. Select the whole wheat setting, then select light/medium crust and start.
4. Once the loaf is done, remove the loaf pan from the machine.
5. Allow it to cool for 10 minutes.
6. Slice and serve.

NUTRITION

Calories 317
Carbs 43.6g
Fat 11g
Protein 10.6g

62. GARLIC PARMESAN BREAD

PREPARATION	COOKING	SERVES
5 MIN	3 HOURS AND 45 MIN	10

INGREDIENTS

- Active dry yeast – ¼ oz.
- Sugar– 3 tbsp.
- Kosher salt – 2 tsp.
- Dried oregano – 1 tsp.
- Dried basil – 1 tsp.
- Garlic powder – ½ tsp.
- Parmesan cheese – ½ cup grated
- All-purpose flour – 3 ½ cups
- Garlic – 1 tbsp., minced
- Butter – ¼ cup, melted
- Olive oil – 1/3 cup
- Water – 1 1/3 cups

DIRECTIONS

1. Add water, oil, butter, and garlic into the bread pan.
2. Add remaining ingredients except for yeast to the bread pan.
3. Make a small hole in the flour with your finger and add yeast to the spot.
4. Make sure yeast will not be mixed with any liquids.
5. Select the basic setting, then selects a light crust and start.
6. Once the loaf is done, remove the loaf pan from the machine.
7. Allow it to cool for 10 minutes.
8. Slice and serve.

NUTRITION

Calories 335
Carbs 37.7g
Fat 15.4g
Protein 9.7g

63. CHEESE JALAPENO BREAD

PREPARATION	COOKING	SERVES
5 MIN	120 MIN	10

INGREDIENTS

- Monterey jack cheese — ¼ cup shredded
- Active dry yeast — 2 tsp.
- Butter — 1 ½ tbsp.
- Sugar — 1 ½ tbsp.
- Milk — 3 tbsp.
- Flour — 3 cups.
- Water — 1 cup.
- Jalapeno pepper — 1, minced
- Salt — 1 ½ tsp

DIRECTIONS

1. Begin by adding all fixings to the bread machine pan according to the bread machine manufacturer instructions.
2. Select basic bread setting, then select light/medium crust and start.
3. Once the loaf is done, remove the loaf pan from the machine.
4. Allow it to cool for 10 minutes.
5. Slice and serve.

NUTRITION

Calories 174
Carbs 31.1g
Fat 3.1g
Protein 5.1g

64. ITALIAN HERB CHEESE BREAD

PREPARATION	COOKING	SERVES
5 MIN	3 HOURS	10

INGREDIENTS

- Yeast – 1 ½ tsp.
- Italian herb seasoning – 1 tbsp.
- Brown sugar – 2 tbsp.
- Cheddar cheese – 1 cup., shredded
- Bread flour – 3 cups.
- Butter – 4 tbsp.
- Warm milk – 1 ¼ cups.
- Salt – 2 tsp

DIRECTIONS

1. Add milk into the bread pan.
2. Add remaining ingredients except for yeast to the bread pan.
3. Make a small hole into the flour with your finger and add yeast to the spot.
4. Make sure yeast will not be mixed with any liquids.
5. Select a basic setting, then selects a light crust and start.
6. Once the loaf is done, remove the loaf pan from the machine.
7. Allow it to cool for 10 minutes.
8. Slice and serve.

NUTRITION

Calories 247
Carbs 32.3g
Fat 9.4g
Protein 8g

65. CHEDDAR CHEESE BASIL BREAD

PREPARATION	COOKING	SERVES
10 MIN	25 MIN	8

INGREDIENTS

- 1 cup milk
- One tablespoon melted butter cooled
- One tablespoon sugar
- One teaspoon dried basil
- ¾ cup (3 ounces) shredded sharp Cheddar cheese
- ¾ teaspoon salt
- cups white bread flour
- 1½ teaspoons active dry yeast

DIRECTIONS

1. Preparing the Ingredients. Place the ingredients in your Zojirushi bread machine.
2. Select the Bake cycle. Program the machine for Regular Basic, choose light or medium crust, and then press Start.
3. If the loaf is done, remove the bucket from the machine.
4. Let the loaf cool for 5 minutes.
5. Softly shake the canister to remove the loaf and put it out onto a rack to cool.

NUTRITION

Calories 174
Carbs 31.1g
Fat 3.1g
Protein 5.1g

66. HERB AND PARMESAN CHEESE LOAF

PREPARATION	COOKING	SERVES
10 MIN	25 MIN	8

INGREDIENTS

- cups + 2 tbsp. all-purpose flour
- 1 cup of water
- tbsp. oil
- tbsp. sugar
- tbsp. milk
- 1 tbsp. instant yeast
- 1 tsp. garlic powder
- tbsp. parmesan cheese
- 1 tbsp. fresh basil
- 1 tbsp. fresh oregano
- 1 tbsp. fresh chives or rosemary

DIRECTIONS

1. Preparing the Ingredients. Place all fixings in the bread pan in the liquid-cheese and herb-dry-yeast layering.
2. Put the pan in the Zojirushi bread machine.
3. Select the Bake cycle. Choose Regular Basic Setting.
4. Press start and wait until the loaf is cooked.
5. The machine will start the keep warm mode after the bread is complete.
6. Just allow it to stay in that mode for about 10 minutes before unplugging.
7. Remove the pan and wait for it to cool down for about 10 minutes.

NUTRITION

Calories 174
Carbs 31.1g
Fat 3.1g
Protein 5.1g

67. OLIVE CHEESE BREAD

PREPARATION	COOKING	SERVES
10 MIN	25 MIN	8

INGREDIENTS

- 1 cup milk
- 1½ tablespoons melted butter, cooled
- One teaspoon minced garlic
- 1½ tablespoons sugar
- One teaspoon salt

- cups white bread flour
- ¾ cup (3 ounces) shredded Swiss cheese
- One teaspoon bread machine or instant yeast
- 1/3 cup chopped black olives

DIRECTIONS

1. Preparing the Ingredients. Place the ingredients in your Zojirushi bread machine, tossing the flour with the cheese first.
2. Program the machine for Regular Basic, choose light or medium crust, and press Start.
3. Next, when the loaf is done, you may remove the bucket from the machine.
4. Let the loaf cool for 5 minutes.
5. Mildly shake the pot to eliminate the loaf and turn it out onto a rack to cool.

NUTRITION

Calories 174
Carbs 31.1g
Fat 3.1g
Protein 5.1g

68. BEER AND CHEESE BREAD

PREPARATION	COOKING	SERVES
10 MIN	25 MIN	8

INGREDIENTS

- 3 cups bread or all-purpose flour
- 1 tbsp. instant yeast
- 1 tsp. salt
- 1 tbsp. sugar
- 1 1/2 cup beer at room temperature
- 1/2 cup shredded Monterey cheese
- 1/2 cup shredded Edam cheese

DIRECTIONS

1. Place all elements, except cheeses, in the bread pan in the liquid-dry-yeast layering.
2. Put the pan in the Zojirushi bread machine.
3. Select the Bake cycle. Choose Regular Basic Setting. Press Start.
4. When the kneading process is about to end, add the cheese.
5. Wait until the loaf is cooked.
6. The machine will start the keep warm mode after the bread is complete.
7. Do not forget to let it stay in that mode for about 10 minutes before unplugging.
8. Lastly, remove the pan and let it cool down for about 10 minutes.

NUTRITION

Calories 174
Carbs 31.1g
Fat 3.1g
Protein 5.1g

69. BLUE CHEESE ONION BREAD

PREPARATION	COOKING	SERVES
10 MIN	25 MIN	8

INGREDIENTS

- 1¼ cup water, at 80°F to 90°F
- One egg, at room temperature
- One tablespoon melted butter cooled
- ¼ cup powdered skim milk
- One tablespoon sugar
- ¾ teaspoon salt
- ½ cup (2 ounces) crumbled blue cheese
- One tablespoon dried onion flake
- 3 cups white bread flour
- ¼ cup instant mashed potato flakes
- One teaspoon bread machine or active dry yeast

DIRECTIONS

1. Preparing the Ingredients. Place the ingredients in your Zojirushi bread machine.
2. Program the machine for Regular Basic, select light or medium crust, and press Start.
3. Remove the bucket from the machine.
4. Let the loaf cool for 5 minutes.
5. Gently shake the container to remove the loaf and turn it out onto a rack to cool.

NUTRITION

Calories 174
Carbs 31.1g
Fat 3.1g
Protein 5.1g

70. CHEESE LOAF

PREPARATION	COOKING	SERVES
10 MIN	25 MIN	8

INGREDIENTS

- 1/4 cups flour
- tsp. instant yeast
- 1 3/4 cups water
- tbsp. sugar
- 1 1/2 cup shredded cheddar cheese
- tbsp. parmesan cheese
- 1 tsp. mustard
- 1 tsp. paprika
- tbsp. minced white onion
- 1/3 cup butter

DIRECTIONS

1. Begin through placing all ingredients in the bread pan in the liquid-dry-yeast layering.
2. Put the pan in the Zojirushi bread machine.
3. Select the Bake cycle. Choose Regular Basic Setting and light crust.
4. Press start and wait until the loaf is cooked.
5. The machine will start the keep warm mode after the bread is complete.
6. For about 10 minutes, let the bread stay for 10 minutes in that mode before unplugging.
7. You may now want to remove the pan and let it cool down for about 10 minutes.

NUTRITION

Calories 174
Carbs 31.1g
Fat 3.1g
Protein 5.1g

71. DOUBLE CHEESE BREAD

PREPARATION	COOKING	SERVES
10 MIN	25 MIN	8

INGREDIENTS

- 1¼ cups milk
- One tablespoon butter, melted and cooled
- Two tablespoons sugar
- One teaspoon salt
- ½ teaspoon freshly ground black pepper
- Pinch cayenne pepper
- 1½ cups (6 ounces) shredded aged sharp Cheddar cheese
- ½ cup (2 ounces) shredded or grated

- Parmesan cheese
- cups white bread flour
- 1¼ teaspoons bread machine or instant yeast

DIRECTIONS

1. Preparing the Ingredients. Place the ingredients in your Zojirushi bread machine.
2. Program the machine for Regular Basic, select light or medium crust, and press Start.
3. Now, if the loaf is done, remove the bucket from the machine.
4. Let the loaf cool for 5 minutes.
5. Moderately shake the bucket to transfer the loaf
6. The last step is by putting it out onto a rack to cool.

NUTRITION

Calories 174
Carbs 31.1g
Fat 3.1g
Protein 5.1g

72. THREE CHEESE BREAD

PREPARATION	COOKING	SERVES
10 MIN	25 MIN	8

INGREDIENTS

- cups bread or all-purpose flour
- 1 1/4 cup warm milk
- tbsp. oil
- tbsp. sugar
- 1 tsp. instant yeast or one packet
- 1 cup cheddar cheese
- 1/2 cup parmesan cheese
- 1/2 cup mozzarella cheese

DIRECTIONS

1. Preparing the Ingredients. Place all ingredients in the bread pan with the liquid-dry-yeast layering.
2. Put the pan in the Zojirushi bread machine.
3. Select the Bake cycle. Choose Regular Basic Setting.
4. Press start and wait until the loaf is cooked.
5. The machine will start the keep warm mode after the bread is complete.
6. Let it stay in that mode for approximately 10 minutes before unplugging.
7. Remove the pan and wait for it to cool down for about 10 minutes.

NUTRITION

Calories 174
Carbs 31.1g
Fat 3.1g
Protein 5.1g

73. SPINACH AND FETA WHOLE WHEAT BREAD

PREPARATION	COOKING	SERVES
10 MIN	25 MIN	8

INGREDIENTS

- 2/3 cups whole wheat flour
- 1 1/2 tsp. instant yeast
- 1/4 cup unsalted butter, melted
- 1 cup lukewarm water
- tbsp. sugar
- 1/2 tsp. salt

- 3/4 cups blanched and chopped spinach, fresh
- 1/2 tsp. pepper
- 1/2 tsp. paprika
- 1/3 cup feta cheese, mashed

DIRECTIONS

1. Preparing the Ingredients. Place all ingredients, except spinach, butter, and feta, in the bread pan in the liquid-dry-yeast layering.
2. Put the pan in the Zojirushi bread machine.
3. Select the Bake cycle. Choose Regular Whole Wheat. Press starts.
4. When the dough has gathered, manually add the feta and spinach.
5. Resume and wait until the loaf are cooked. Once cooked, brush with butter.
6. The machine will start the keep warm mode after the bread is complete.
7. Make it stay in that mode for about 10 minutes before unplugging.
8. Remove the pan and just cool it down for about 10 minutes.

NUTRITION

Calories 174
Carbs 31.1g
Fat 3.1g
Protein 5.1g

74. MOZZARELLA AND SALAMI BREAD

PREPARATION	COOKING	SERVES
10 MIN	25 MIN	8

INGREDIENTS

- 1 cup water plus two tablespoons, at 80°F to 90°F
- ½ cup (2 ounces) shredded mozzarella cheese
- Two tablespoons sugar
- One teaspoon salt
- One teaspoon dried basil
- ¼ teaspoon garlic powder
- 3¼ cups white bread flour
- 1½ teaspoons bread machine or instant yeast
- ¾ cup finely diced hot German salami

DIRECTIONS

1. Preparing the Ingredients. Place the ingredients, except the salami, in your Zojirushi bread machine.
2. Program the machine for Regular Basic, select light or medium crust, and press Start.
3. Add the salami when your machine signals or 5 minutes before the second kneading cycle is finished.
4. You need to remove the bucket from the machine.
5. Next is by letting the loaf cool for 5 minutes.
6. Gently shake the bucket to eliminate the loaf and turn it out onto a rack to cool.

NUTRITION

Calories 174
Carbs 31.1g
Fat 3.1g
Protein 5.1g

75. CHEESE SWIRL LOAF

PREPARATION	COOKING	SERVES
15 MIN	25 MIN	8

INGREDIENTS

- cups all-purpose flour
- 1 1/4 cup lukewarm milk
- tbsp. sugar
- 1 tsp. salt
- 1 1/2 tsp. instant yeast
- tbsp. melted butter
- Four slices of Monterey cheese
- 1/2 cup mozzarella cheese
- 1/2 cup edam or any quick melting cheese
- 1/2 tsp. paprika

DIRECTIONS

1. Preparing the Ingredients. Place all ingredients, except cheeses, in the bread pan in the liquid-dry-yeast layering.
2. Put the pan in the Zojirushi bread machine.
3. Select the Bake cycle. Choose Regular Basic Setting. Press starts.
4. Place all the cheese in a microwavable bowl. Melt in the microwave for 30 seconds. Cool, but make sure to keep soft.
5. After 10 minutes into the kneading process, pause the machine. Take out half of the dough. Roll it flat on the work surface.
6. Spread the cheese on the flat dough, then roll it thinly. Return to the bread pan carefully.
7. Resume and wait until the loaf are cooked.
8. The machine will start the keep warm mode after the bread is complete.
9. Let it stay in that mode for about 10 minutes before unplugging.
10. To end by removing the pan and let it cool down for about 10 minutes.

NUTRITION

Calories 174
Carbs 31.1g
Fat 3.1g
Protein 5.1g

76. CHILI CHEESE BACON BREAD

PREPARATION	COOKING	SERVES
10 MIN	25 MIN	8

INGREDIENTS

- ½ cup milk
- 1½ teaspoons melted butter, cooled
- 1½ tablespoons honey
- 1½ teaspoons salt
- ½ cup chopped and drained green chiles
- ½ cup (2 ounces) grated Cheddar cheese
- ½ cup chopped cooked bacon
- cups white bread flour
- Two teaspoons bread machine or instant yeast

DIRECTIONS

1. Preparing the Ingredients. Place the ingredients in your Zojirushi bread machine.
2. Select the Bake cycle. Program the machine for Regular Basic, select light or medium crust, and press Start.
3. Remove the bucket from the machine.
4. Let the loaf cool for 5 minutes.
5. Gently swing the can to remove the loaf and put it out onto a rack to cool.

NUTRITION

Calories 174
Carbs 31.1g
Fat 3.1g
Protein 5.1g

SPICE & HERB BREAD

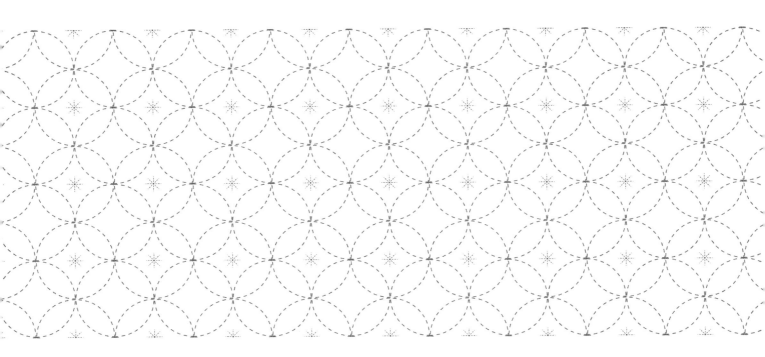

77. HERBAL GARLIC CREAM CHEESE DELIGHT

PREPARATION	COOKING	SERVES	DIFFICULTY
5 MIN	2 HOURS 45 MIN	8 SLICES	INTERMEDIATE

INGREDIENTS

- 1/3 cup water at 80 degrees F
- 1/3 cup herb and garlic cream cheese mix, at room temp
- 1 whole egg, beaten, at room temp
- 4 teaspoons melted butter, cooled
- 1 tablespoon sugar
- 2/3 teaspoon salt
- 2 cups white bread flour
- 1 teaspoon instant yeast

NUTRITION

Total Carbs: 27g
Fiber: 2g
Protein: 5g
Fat: 6g
Calories: 182

DIRECTIONS

1. Add all of the ingredients to your bread machine, carefully following the instructions of the manufacturer.
2. Set the program of your bread machine to Basic/White Bread and set crust type to Medium.
3. Wait until the cycle completes.
4. Once the loaf is ready, take the bucket out and let the loaf cool for 5 minutes.
5. Gently shake the bucket to remove the loaf.

78. CUMIN TOSSED FANCY BREAD

PREPARATION	COOKING	SERVES	DIFFICULTY
5 MIN	3 HOURS 15 MIN	16 SLICES	INTERMEDIATE

INGREDIENTS

- 5 1/3 cups wheat flour
- 1½ teaspoons salt
- 1½ tablespoons sugar
- 1 tablespoon dry yeast
- 1¾ cups water
- 2 tablespoons cumin
- 3 tablespoons sunflower oil

NUTRITION

Total Carbs: 67g
Fiber: 2g
Protein: 9.5g
Fat: 7g
Calories: 368

DIRECTIONS

1. Add warm water to the bread machine bucket.
2. Add salt, sugar, and sunflower oil.
3. Sift in wheat flour and add yeast.
4. Set the program of your bread machine to French bread and set crust type to Medium.
5. Once the maker beeps, add cumin.
6. Wait until the cycle completes.
7. Once the loaf is ready, take the bucket out and let the loaf cool for 5 minutes.
8. Gently shake the bucket to remove the loaf.

79. POTATO ROSEMARY LOAF

PREPARATION	COOKING	SERVES	DIFFICULTY
5 MIN	3 HOURS 25 MIN	20 SLICES	INTERMEDIATE

INGREDIENTS

- 4 cups wheat flour
- 1 tablespoon sugar
- 1 tablespoon sunflower oil
- 1½ teaspoons salt
- 1½ cups water

- 1 teaspoon dry yeast
- 1 cup mashed potatoes, ground through a sieve
- crushed rosemary to taste

NUTRITION

Total Carbs: 54g
Fiber: 1g
Protein: 8g
Fat: 3g
Calories: 276

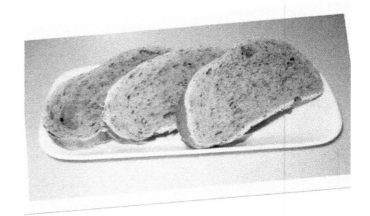

DIRECTIONS

1. Add flour, salt, and sugar to the bread maker bucket and attach mixing paddle.
2. Add sunflower oil and water.
3. Put in yeast as directed.
4. Set the program of your bread machine to Bread with Filling mode and set crust type to Medium.
5. Once the bread maker beeps and signals to add more ingredients, open lid, add mashed potatoes, and chopped rosemary.
6. Wait until the cycle completes.
7. Once the loaf is ready, take the bucket out and let the loaf cool for 5 minutes.
8. Gently shake the bucket to remove the loaf.

80. DELICIOUS HONEY LAVENDER BREAD

PREPARATION	COOKING	SERVES	DIFFICULTY
10 MIN	3 HOURS 25 MIN	16 SLICES	INTERMEDIATE

INGREDIENTS

- 1½ cups wheat flour
- 2 1/3 cups whole meal flour
- 1 teaspoon fresh yeast
- 1½ cups water
- 1 teaspoon lavender
- 1½ tablespoons honey
- 1 teaspoon salt

NUTRITION

Total Carbs: 46g
Fiber: 1g
Protein: 7.5g
Fat: 1.5g
Calories: 226

DIRECTIONS

1. Sift both types of flour in a bowl and mix.
2. Add all of the ingredients to your bread machine, carefully following the instructions of the manufacturer.
3. Set the program of your bread machine to Basic/White Bread and set crust type to Medium.
4. Wait until the cycle completes.
5. Once the loaf is ready, take the bucket out and let the loaf cool for 5 minutes.
6. Gently shake the bucket to remove the loaf.

81. INSPIRING CINNAMON BREAD

PREPARATION	COOKING	SERVES	DIFFICULTY
5 MIN	2 HOURS 15 MIN	8 SLICES	INTERMEDIATE

INGREDIENTS

- 2/3 cup milk at 80 degrees F
- 1 whole egg, beaten
- 3 tablespoons melted butter, cooled
- 1/3 cup sugar
- 1/3 teaspoon salt
- 1 teaspoon ground cinnamon
- 2 cups white bread flour
- 1 1/3 teaspoons active dry yeast

NUTRITION

Total Carbs: 34g
Fiber: 1g
Protein: 5g
Fat: 5g
Calories: 198

DIRECTIONS

1. Add all of the ingredients to your bread machine, carefully following the instructions of the manufacturer.
2. Set the program of your bread machine to Basic/White Bread and set crust type to Medium.
3. Wait until the cycle completes.
4. Once the loaf is ready, take the bucket out and let the loaf cool for 5 minutes.
5. Remove the loaf

82. LAVENDER BUTTERMILK BREAD

PREPARATION	COOKING	SERVES	DIFFICULTY
10 MIN	3 HOURS	14	EXPERT

INGREDIENTS

- ½ cup water
- 7/8 cup buttermilk
- 1/4 cup olive oil
- 3 Tablespoon finely chopped fresh lavender leaves
- 1 ¼ teaspoon finely chopped fresh lavender flowers

- Grated zest of 1 lemon
- 4 cups bread flour
- 2 teaspoon salt
- 2 3/4 teaspoon bread machine yeast

NUTRITION

Carbs: 27 g
Fat: 5 g
Protein: 2 g
Calories: 170

DIRECTIONS

1. Add each ingredient to the bread machine in the order and at the temperature recommended by your bread machine manufacturer.
2. Close the lid, select the basic bread, medium crust setting on your bread machine and press start.
3. When the bread machine has finished baking, remove the bread and put it on a cooling rack.

83. CAJUN BREAD

PREPARATION	COOKING	SERVES	DIFFICULTY
10 MIN	2 HOURS 10 MIN	14	INTERMEDIATE

INGREDIENTS

- ½ cup water
- ¼ cup chopped onion
- ¼ cup chopped green bell pepper
- 2 teaspoon finely chopped garlic
- 2 teaspoon soft butter
- 2 cups bread flour
- 1 Tablespoon sugar
- 1 teaspoon Cajun
- ½ teaspoon salt
- 1 teaspoon active dry yeast

NUTRITION

Carbs: 23 g
Fat: 4 g
Protein: 5 g
Calories: 150

DIRECTIONS

1. Add each ingredient to the bread machine in the order and at the temperature recommended by your bread machine manufacturer.
2. Close the lid, select the basic bread, medium crust setting on your bread machine and press start.
3. When the bread machine has finished baking, remove the bread and put it on a cooling rack.

84. TURMERIC BREAD

PREPARATION	COOKING	SERVES	DIFFICULTY
5 MIN	3 HOURS	14	INTERMEDIATE

INGREDIENTS

- 1 teaspoon dried yeast
- 4 cups strong white flour
- 1 teaspoon turmeric powder
- 2 teaspoon beetroot powder
- 2 Tablespoon olive oil
- 1.5 teaspoon salt
- 1 teaspoon chili flakes
- 1 3/8 water

NUTRITION

Carbs: 24 g
Fat: 3 g
Protein: 2 g
Calories: 129

DIRECTIONS

1. Add each ingredient to the bread machine in the order and at the temperature recommended by your bread machine manufacturer.
2. Close the lid, select the basic bread, medium crust setting on your bread machine and press start.
3. When the bread machine has finished baking, remove the bread and put it on a cooling rack.

85. ROSEMARY CRANBERRY PECAN BREAD

PREPARATION	COOKING	SERVES	DIFFICULTY
30 MIN	3 HOURS	14	INTERMEDIATE

INGREDIENTS

- 1 1/3 cups water, plus
- 2 Tablespoon water
- 2 Tablespoon butter
- 2 teaspoon salt
- 4 cups bread flour
- 3/4 cup dried sweetened cranberries
- 3/4 cup toasted chopped pecans
- 2 Tablespoon non-fat powdered milk
- ¼ cup sugar
- 2 teaspoon yeast

NUTRITION

Carbs: 18 g
Fat: 5 g
Protein: 9 g
Calories: 120

DIRECTIONS

1. Add each ingredient to the bread machine in the order and at the temperature recommended by your bread machine manufacturer.
2. Close the lid, select the basic bread, medium crust setting on your bread machine and press start.
3. When the bread machine has finished baking, remove the bread and put it on a cooling rack.

86. SESAME FRENCH BREAD

PREPARATION	COOKING	SERVES	DIFFICULTY
20 MIN	3 HOURS 15 MIN	14	INTERMEDIATE

INGREDIENTS

- 7/8 cup water
- 1 Tablespoon butter, softened
- 3 cups bread flour
- 2 teaspoon sugar
- 1 teaspoon salt
- 2 teaspoon yeast
- 2 Tablespoon sesame seeds toasted

NUTRITION

Carbs: 28 g
Fat: 3 g
Protein: 6 g
Calories: 180

DIRECTIONS

1. Add each ingredient to the bread machine in the order and at the temperature recommended by your bread machine manufacturer.
2. Close the lid, select the French bread, medium crust setting on your bread machine and press start.
3. When the bread machine has finished baking, remove the bread and put it on a cooling rack.

87. HERB BREAD

PREPARATION	COOKING	SERVES	DIFFICULTY
80 MIN	50 MIN (20+30 MIN)	1 LOAF	INTERMEDIATE

INGREDIENTS

- 3/4 to 7/8 cup milk
- 1 tablespoon Sugar
- 1 teaspoon Salt
- tablespoon Butter or margarine
- 1/3 cup chopped onion
- cups bread flour
- 1/2 teaspoon Dried dill
- 1/2 teaspoon Dried basil
- 1/2 teaspoon Dried rosemary
- 11/2 teaspoon Active dry yeast

DIRECTIONS

1. Place all the Ingredients in the bread pan. Select medium crus then the rapid bake cycle. Press starts.
2. After 5-10 minutes, observe the dough as it kneads, if you hear straining sounds in your machine or if the dough appears stiff and dry, add 1 tablespoon Liquid at a time until the dough becomes smooth, pliable, soft, and slightly tacky to the touch.
3. Remove the bread from the pan after baking. Place on rack and allow to cool for 1 hour before slicing.

NUTRITION

Calories: 65 Cal
Fat 0 g
Carbohydrates:13 g
Protein 2 g

88. ROSEMARY WHITE BREAD

PREPARATION	COOKING	SERVES	DIFFICULTY
2 HOURS 10 MIN	50 MIN	1 LOAF	INTERMEDIATE

INGREDIENTS

- ¾ cup + 1 tablespoon water at 80 degrees F
- 1⅔ tablespoons melted butter, cooled
- teaspoons sugar
- 1 teaspoon salt
- 1 tablespoon fresh rosemary, chopped
- cups white bread flour
- 1⅓ teaspoons instant yeast

DIRECTIONS

1. Add all of the ingredients to your bread machine, carefully following the instructions of the manufacturer.
2. Set the program of your bread machine to Basic/White Bread and set crust type to Medium.
3. Press START.
4. Wait until the cycle completes.
5. Once the loaf is ready, take the bucket out and let the loaf cool for 5 minutes.
6. Gently shake the bucket to remove the loaf.
7. Transfer to a cooling rack, slice, and serve.

NUTRITION

Calories: 142 Cal
Fat: 3 g
Carbohydrates:25 g
Protein: 4 g
Fiber: 1 g

89. ORIGINAL ITALIAN HERB BREAD

PREPARATION	COOKING	SERVES	DIFFICULTY
2 HOURS 40 MIN	50 MIN	2 LOAVES	INTERMEDIATE

INGREDIENTS

- 1 cup water at 80 degrees F
- ½ cup olive brine
- 1½ tablespoons butter
- tablespoons sugar
- teaspoons salt
- 5⅓ cups flour
- teaspoons bread machine yeast
- 20 olives, black/green
- 1½ teaspoons Italian herbs

DIRECTIONS

1. Cut olives into slices.
2. Add all of the ingredients to your bread machine (except olives), carefully following the instructions of the manufacturer.
3. Set the program of your bread machine to French bread and set crust type to Medium.
4. Press START.
5. Once the maker beeps, add olives.
6. Wait until the cycle completes.
7. Once the loaf is ready, take the bucket out and let the loaf cool for 5 minutes.
8. Gently shake the bucket to remove the loaf.
9. Transfer to a cooling rack, slice, and serve.

NUTRITION

Calories: 386 Cal
Fat: 7 g
Carbohydrates: 71 g
Protein: 10 g
Fiber: 1 g

90. LOVELY AROMATIC LAVENDER BREAD

PREPARATION	COOKING	SERVES	DIFFICULTY
2 HOURS 10 MIN	50 MIN	1 LOAF	INTERMEDIATE

INGREDIENTS

- ¾ cup milk at 80 degrees F
- 1 tablespoon melted butter, cooled
- 1 tablespoon sugar
- ¾ teaspoon salt
- 1 teaspoon fresh lavender flower, chopped
- ¼ teaspoon lemon zest
- ¼ teaspoon fresh thyme, chopped
- cups white bread flour
- ¾ teaspoon instant yeast

DIRECTIONS

1. Add all of the ingredients to your bread machine
2. Set the program of your bread machine to Basic/White Bread and set crust type to Medium.
3. Press START.
4. Wait until the cycle completes.
5. Once the loaf is ready, take the bucket out and let the loaf cool for 5 minutes.
6. Gently shake the bucket to remove the loaf.
7. Transfer to a cooling rack, slice, and serve.

NUTRITION

Calories: 144 Cal
Fat: 2 g
Carbohydrates: 27 g
Protein: 4 g
Fiber: 1 g

91. OREGANO MOZZA-CHEESE BREAD

PREPARATION	COOKING	SERVES	DIFFICULTY
20 HOURS 50 MIN	50 MIN	2 LOAVES	INTERMEDIATE

INGREDIENTS

- 1 cup (milk + egg) mixture
- ½ cup mozzarella cheese
- 2¼ cups flour
- ¾ cup whole grain flour
- tablespoons sugar
- 1 teaspoon salt
- teaspoons oregano
- 1½ teaspoons dry yeast

DIRECTIONS

1. Add all of the ingredients to your bread machine
2. Set the program of your bread machine to Basic/White Bread and set crust type to Dark.
3. Press START.
4. Wait until the cycle completes.
5. Once the loaf is ready, take the bucket out and let the loaf cool for 5 minutes.
6. Gently shake the bucket to remove the loaf.
7. Transfer to a cooling rack, slice, and serve.

NUTRITION

Calories: 209 Cal
Fat: 2.1 g
Carbohydrates: 40 g
Protein: 7.7 g
Fiber: 1 g

92. GARLIC BREAD

PREPARATION	COOKING	SERVES	DIFFICULTY
2 HOURS 30 MIN	40 MIN	1 LOAF	INTERMEDIATE

INGREDIENTS

- 1 3/8 cups water
- tablespoons olive oil
- 1 teaspoon minced garlic
- cups bread flour
- tablespoons white sugar
- teaspoons salt

- 1/4 cup grated Parmesan cheese
- 1 teaspoon dried basil
- 1 teaspoon garlic powder
- tablespoons chopped fresh chives
- 1 teaspoon coarsely ground black pepper
- 1/2 teaspoons bread machine yeast

DIRECTIONS

1. Follow the order of putting the ingredients into the pan of the bread machine recommended by the manufacturer.
2. Choose the Basic or the White Bread cycle on the machine and press the Start button.

NUTRITION

Calories: 175 calories;
Total Carbohydrate: 29.7 g
Cholesterol: 1 mg

Total Fat: 3.7 g
Protein: 5.2 g
Sodium: 332 mg

93. ROSEMARY BREAD

PREPARATION	COOKING	SERVES	DIFFICULTY
2 HOURS 40 MIN	25-30 MIN	1 LOAF	INTERMEDIATE

INGREDIENTS

- 1 cup water
- tablespoons olive oil
- 1 1/2 teaspoons white sugar
- 1 1/2 teaspoons salt
- 1/4 teaspoon Italian seasoning
- 1/4 teaspoon ground black pepper
- 1 tablespoon dried rosemary
- 1/2 cups bread flour
- 1 1/2 teaspoons active dry yeast

DIRECTIONS

1. Into the bread machine pan, put the ingredients following the order recommended by manufacturer.
2. Use the white bread cycle and then push the Start button.

NUTRITION

Calories: 137 calories;
Total Carbohydrate: 21.6 g
Cholesterol: 0 mg

Total Fat: 3.9 g
Protein: 3.6 g
Sodium: 292 mg

94. CUMIN BREAD

PREPARATION	COOKING	SERVES	DIFFICULTY
3 HOURS 30 MIN	15 MIN	8	INTERMEDIATE

INGREDIENTS

- 1/3 cups bread machine flour, sifted
- 1½ teaspoon kosher salt
- 1½ Tablespoon sugar
- 1 Tablespoon bread machine yeast
- 1¾ cups lukewarm water
- Tablespoon black cumin
- Tablespoon sunflower oil

DIRECTIONS

1. Place all the dry and liquid ingredients in the pan and follow the instructions for your bread machine.
2. Set the baking program to BASIC and the crust type to MEDIUM.
3. If the dough is too dense or too wet, adjust the amount of flour and liquid in the recipe.
4. When the program has ended, take the pan out of the bread machine and let cool for 5 minutes.
5. Shake the loaf out of the pan. If necessary, use a spatula.
6. Wrap the bread with a kitchen towel and set it aside for an hour. Otherwise, you can cool it on a wire rack.

NUTRITION

Calories: 368 calories;
Total Carbohydrate: 67.1 g
Cholesterol: 0 mg
Total Fat: 6.5 g

Protein: 9.5 g
Sodium: 444 mg
Sugar: 2.5 g

95. SAFFRON TOMATO BREAD

PREPARATION	COOKING	SERVES	DIFFICULTY
3 HOURS 30 MIN	15 MIN	10	INTERMEDIATE

INGREDIENTS

- 1 teaspoon bread machine yeast
- 2½ cups wheat bread machine flour
- 1 Tablespoon panifarin
- 1½ teaspoon kosher salt
- 1½ Tablespoon white sugar
- Tablespoon extra-virgin olive oil

- Tablespoon tomatoes, dried and chopped
- 1 Tablespoon tomato paste
- ½ cup firm cheese (cubes)
- ½ cup feta cheese
- 1 pinch saffron
- 1½ cups serum

DIRECTIONS

1. Five minutes before cooking, pour in dried tomatoes and 1 tablespoon of olive oil. Add the tomato paste and mix.
2. Place all the dry and liquid ingredients, except additives, in the pan and follow the instructions for your bread machine.
3. Pay particular attention to measuring the ingredients. Use a measuring cup, measuring spoon, and kitchen scales to do so.
4. Set the baking program to BASIC and the crust type to MEDIUM.
5. Add the additives after the beep or place them in the dispenser of the bread machine.
6. Shake the loaf out of the pan. If necessary, use a spatula.
7. Wrap the bread with a kitchen towel and set it aside for an hour. Otherwise, you can cool it on a wire rack.

NUTRITION

Calories: 260 calories;
Total Carbohydrate: 35.5 g
Cholesterol: 20 g
Total Fat: 9.2g

Protein: 8.9 g
Sodium: 611 mg
Sugar: 5.2 g

96. CRACKED BLACK PEPPER BREAD

PREPARATION	COOKING	SERVES	DIFFICULTY
3 HOURS 30 MIN	15 MIN	8	INTERMEDIATE

INGREDIENTS

- ¾ cup water, at 80°F to 90°F
- 1 tablespoon melted butter, cooled
- 1 tablespoon sugar
- ¾ teaspoon salt
- tablespoons skim milk powder
- 1 tablespoon minced chives
- ½ teaspoon garlic powder
- ½ teaspoon cracked black pepper
- cups white bread flour
- ¾ teaspoon bread machine or instant yeast

DIRECTIONS

1. Place the ingredients in your bread machine as recommended by the manufacturer.
2. Program the machine for Basic/White bread, select light or medium crust, and press Start.
3. When the loaf is done, remove the bucket from the machine.
4. Let the loaf cool for 5 minutes.
5. Gently shake the bucket to remove the loaf, and turn it out onto a rack to cool.

NUTRITION

Calories: 141 calories;
Total Carbohydrate: 27 g
Total Fat: 2g

Protein: 4 g
Sodium: 215 mg
Fiber: 1 g

97. SPICY CAJUN BREAD

PREPARATION	COOKING	SERVES	DIFFICULTY
2 HOUR	15 MIN	8	INTERMEDIATE

INGREDIENTS

- ¾ cup water, at 80°F to 90°F
- 1 tablespoon melted butter, cooled
- teaspoons tomato paste
- 1 tablespoon sugar
- 1 teaspoon salt
- tablespoons skim milk powder
- ½ tablespoon Cajun seasoning
- ⅛ teaspoon onion powder
- cups white bread flour
- 1 teaspoon bread machine or instant yeast

DIRECTIONS

1. Place the ingredients in your bread machine as recommended by the manufacturer.
2. Program the machine for Basic/White bread, select light or medium crust, and press Start.
3. When the loaf is done, remove the bucket from the machine.
4. Let the loaf cool for 5 minutes.
5. Gently shake the bucket to remove the loaf, and turn it out onto a rack to cool.

NUTRITION

Calories: 141 calories;
Total Carbohydrate: 27 g
Total Fat: 2g

Protein: 4 g
Sodium: 215 mg
Fiber: 1 g

98. ANISE LEMON BREAD

PREPARATION	COOKING	SERVES	DIFFICULTY
2 HOURS	15 MIN	8	INTERMEDIATE

INGREDIENTS

- ⅔ Cup water, at 80°F to 90°F
- 1 egg, at room temperature
- 2⅔ tablespoons butter, melted and cooled
- 2⅔ tablespoons honey
- ⅓ Teaspoon salt
- ⅔ Teaspoon anise seed
- ⅔ Teaspoon lemon zest
- cups white bread flour
- 1⅓ teaspoons bread machine or instant yeast

DIRECTIONS

1. Place the ingredients in your bread machine as recommended by the manufacturer.
2. Program the machine for Basic/White bread, select light or medium crust, and press Start.
3. When the loaf is done, remove the bucket from the machine.
4. Let the loaf cool for 5 minutes.
5. Gently shake the bucket to remove the loaf, and turn it out onto a rack to cool.

NUTRITION

Calories: 158 calories;
Total Carbohydrate: 27 g
Total Fat: 5g

Protein: 4 g
Sodium: 131 mg
Fiber: 1 g

99. CARDAMON BREAD

PREPARATION	COOKING	SERVES	DIFFICULTY
2 HOURS	15 MIN	8	INTERMEDIATE

INGREDIENTS

- ½ cup milk, at 80°F to 90°F
- 1 egg, at room temperature
- 1 teaspoon melted butter, cooled
- teaspoons honey
- ⅔ Teaspoon salt
- ⅔ Teaspoon ground cardamom
- cups white bread flour
- ¾ teaspoon bread machine or instant yeast

DIRECTIONS

1. Place the ingredients in your bread machine as recommended by the manufacturer.
2. Program the machine for Basic/White bread, select light or medium crust, and press Start.
3. When the loaf is done, remove the bucket from the machine.
4. Let the loaf cool for 5 minutes.
5. Gently shake the bucket to remove the loaf, and turn it out onto a rack to cool.

NUTRITION

Calories: 149 calories;
Total Carbohydrate: 29 g
Total Fat: 2g

Protein: 5 g
Sodium: 211 mg
Fiber: 1 g

GLUTEN-FREE BREAD

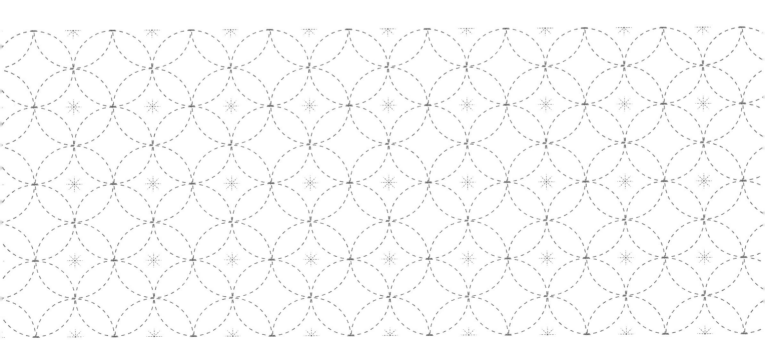

100. GLUTEN-FREE WHITE BREAD

PREPARATION	COOKING	SERVES
10 MIN	25 MIN	8

INGREDIENTS

- 2 cups white rice flour
- 1 cup potato starch
- 1/2 cup soy flour
- 1/2 cup cornstarch
- 1 tsp. vinegar
- 1 tsp. xanthan gum
- 1 tsp. instant yeast (bread yeast should be gluten-free, but always check)
- 1 1/4 cup buttermilk
- Three eggs
- 1/4 cup sugar or honey
- 1/4 cup coconut or olive oil

DIRECTIONS

1. Place all ingredients in the Cuisinart bread pan in the liquid-dry-yeast layering.
2. Put the pan in the Cuisinart bread machine.
3. Select the Bake cycle. Choose Gluten Free. Press Start.
4. Five minutes into the kneading process, pause the machine and check the firmness of the dough. Add more flour if necessary.
5. Resume and wait until the loaf are cooked.
6. The machine will start the keep warm mode after the bread is complete.
7. Allow it to stay in that mode for about 10 minutes before unplugging.
8. Remove the pan and let it cool down for about 10 minutes.

NUTRITION

Calories: 151
Sodium: 265 mg
Dietary Fiber: 4.3 g

Fat: 4.5 g
Carbs: 27.2 g
Protein: 3.5 g

101. BROWN RICE BREAD

PREPARATION	COOKING	SERVES
10 MIN	25 MIN	8

INGREDIENTS

- brown rice flour
- Two eggs
- 1 1/4 cup almond milk
- 1 tsp. vinegar
- 1/2 cup coconut oil
- 2 tbsp. sugar
- 1/2 tsp. salt
- 2 1/4 tsp. instant yeast

DIRECTIONS

1. Place all ingredients in the Cuisinart bread pan in the liquid-dry-yeast layering.
2. Put the pan in the Cuisinart bread machine.
3. Select the Bake cycle. Choose Gluten-free. Press Start.
4. Five minutes into the kneading process, pause the machine, and check the consistency of the dough. Add more flour if necessary.
5. Resume and wait until the loaf are cooked.
6. The machine will start the keep warm mode after the bread is complete.
7. Make it stay in that mode for about 10 minutes before unplugging.
8. Remove the pan and let it cool down for about 10 minutes.

NUTRITION

Calories: 151
Sodium: 265 mg
Dietary Fiber: 4.3 g

Fat: 4.5 g
Carbs: 27.2 g
Protein: 3.5 g

102. BROWN RICE AND CRANBERRY BREAD

PREPARATION	COOKING	SERVES
10 MIN	25 MIN	8

INGREDIENTS

- Three eggs, beaten
- 1 tsp. white vinegar
- 3 tbsp. gluten-free oil
- 1 1/2 cup lukewarm water
- 3 cups brown rice flour
- 1 tbsp. xanthan gum
- 1/4 cup flaxseed meal
- 1 tsp. salt
- 1/4 cup sugar
- 1/2 cup powdered milk
- 2/3 cup cranberries, dried and cut into bits
- 2 1/4 tsp. instant yeast (bread yeast should be gluten-free, but always check)

DIRECTIONS

1. Preparing the Ingredients. Mix all the wet and the dry ingredients, except the yeast and cranberries, separately.
2. Place all ingredients in the Cuisinart bread pan in the liquid-dry-yeast layering.
3. Put the pan in the Cuisinart bread machine.
4. Load the cranberries in the automatic dispenser.
5. Select the Bake cycle. Choose Gluten-free. Press start and wait until the loaf is cooked.
6. The machine will start the keep warm mode after the bread is complete.
7. Let it stay in that mode for around 10 minutes before unplugging.
8. Remove the pan and let it cool down for about 10 minutes. Layer them in the bread machine, in the liquid-dry-yeast layering. Do not add the cranberries.

NUTRITION

Calories: 151
Sodium: 265 mg
Dietary Fiber: 4.3 g

Fat: 4.5 g
Carbs: 27.2 g
Protein: 3.5 g

103. GLUTEN-FREE PEASANT BREAD

PREPARATION	COOKING	SERVES
10 MIN	25 MIN	8

INGREDIENTS

- 2 cups brown rice flour
- 1 cup potato starch
- 1 tbsp. xanthan gum
- 2 tbsp. sugar

- 2 tbsp. yeast (bread yeast should be gluten-free, but always check)
- 3 tbsp. vegetable oil
- Five eggs
- 1 tsp. white vinegar

DIRECTIONS

1. Preparing the Ingredients. Bloom the yeast in water with the sugar for five minutes.
2. Place all ingredients in the Cuisinart bread pan in the yeast-liquid-dry layering.
3. Put the pan in the Cuisinart bread machine.
4. Select the Bake cycle. Choose Gluten Free. Press start and stand by until the loaf is cooked.
5. The machine will start the keep warm mode after the bread is complete.
6. Let it stay in that mode for approximately 10 minutes before unplugging.
7. Remove the pan and let it cool down for about 10 minutes.

NUTRITION

Calories: 151
Sodium: 265 mg
Dietary Fiber: 4.3 g
Fat: 4.5 g
Carbs: 27.2 g
Protein: 3.5 g

104. GLUTEN-FREE HAWAIIAN LOAF

PREPARATION	COOKING	SERVES
10 MIN	25 MIN	8

INGREDIENTS

- 4 cups gluten-free four
- 1 tsp. xanthan gum
- 2 1/2 tsp. (bread yeast should be gluten-free, but always check)
- 1/4 cup white sugar
- 1/2 cup softened butter
- One egg, beaten
- 1 cup fresh pineapple juice, warm
- 1/2 tsp. salt
- 1 tsp. vanilla extract

DIRECTIONS

1. Place all ingredients in the Cuisinart bread pan in the liquid-dry-yeast layering.
2. Put the pan in the Cuisinart bread machine.
3. Select the Bake cycle. Choose Gluten Free. Press open and wait until the loaf is cooked.
4. The machine will start the keep warm mode after the bread is complete.
5. Let it stay in that mode for 10 minutes before unplugging.
6. Remove the pan and let it cool down for about 10 minutes.

NUTRITION

Calories: 151
Sodium: 265 mg
Dietary Fiber: 4.3 g

Fat: 4.5 g
Carbs: 27.2 g
Protein: 3.5 g

105. VEGAN GLUTEN-FREE BREAD

PREPARATION	COOKING	SERVES
10 MIN	25 MIN	8

INGREDIENTS

- 1 cup almond flour
- 1 cup brown or white rice flour
- 2 tbsp. potato flour
- 4 tsp. baking powder
- 1/4 tsp. baking soda
- 1 cup almond milk
- 1 tbsp. white vinegar

DIRECTIONS

1. Place all ingredients in the Cuisinart bread pan in the liquid-dry-yeast layering.
2. Put the pan in the Cuisinart bread machine.
3. Select the Bake cycle. Choose Gluten Free.
4. Press start and wait until the loaf is cooked.
5. The machine will start the keep warm mode after the bread is complete.
6. Let it stay in that mode for at least 10 minutes before unplugging.
7. Remove the pan and let it cool down for about 10 minutes.

NUTRITION

Calories: 151
Sodium: 265 mg
Dietary Fiber: 4.3 g

Fat: 4.5 g
Carbs: 27.2 g
Protein: 3.5 g

106. GLUTEN-FREE SIMPLE SANDWICH BREAD

PREPARATION	COOKING	SERVES
5 MIN	60 MIN	12

INGREDIENTS

- 1 1/2 cups sorghum flour
- 1 cup tapioca starch or potato starch
- 1/3 cup gluten-free millet flour or gluten-free oat flour
- Two teaspoons xanthan gum
- 1 1/4 teaspoons fine sea salt
- 2 1/2 teaspoons gluten-free yeast for bread machines

- 1 1/4 cups warm water
- Three tablespoons extra virgin olive oil
- One tablespoon honey or raw agave nectar
- 1/2 teaspoon mild rice vinegar or lemon juice
- Two organic free-range eggs, beaten

DIRECTIONS

1. Blend the dry ingredients except for the yeast and set aside.
2. Add the liquid ingredients to the bread maker pan first, then gently pour the mixed dry ingredients on top of the liquid.
3. Make a well in the center part of the dry ingredients and add the yeast.
4. Set for Rapid 1 hour 20 minutes, medium crust color, and press Start.
5. In the end, put it on a cooling rack for 15 minutes before slicing to serve.

NUTRITION

Calories: 137
Sodium: 85 mg
Dietary Fiber: 2.7 g

Fat: 4.6 g
Carbs: 22.1 g
Protein: 2.4 g

107. GRAIN-FREE CHIA BREAD

PREPARATION	COOKING	SERVES
3 MIN	3 HOURS	12

INGREDIENTS

- 1 cup of warm water
- Three large organic eggs, room temperature
- 1/4 cup olive oil
- One tablespoon apple cider vinegar
- 1 cup gluten-free chia seeds, ground to flour
- 1 cup almond meal flour
- 1/2 cup potato starch
- 1/4 cup coconut flour
- 3/4 cup millet flour
- One tablespoon xanthan gum
- 1 1/2 teaspoons salt
- Two tablespoons sugar
- Three tablespoons nonfat dry milk
- Six teaspoons instant yeast

DIRECTIONS

1. Whisk wet ingredients together and place it in the bread maker pan.
2. Whisk dry ingredients, except yeast, together, and add on top of wet ingredients.
3. Make a well in the dry ingredients and add yeast.
4. Select the Whole Wheat cycle, light crust color, and press Start.
5. Allow cooling completely before serving.

NUTRITION

Calories: 375
Sodium: 462 mg
Dietary Fiber: 22.3 g

Fat: 18.3 g
Carbs: 42 g
Protein: 12.2 g

108. GLUTEN-FREE BROWN BREAD

PREPARATION	COOKING	SERVES
5 MIN	3 HOURS	12

INGREDIENTS

- Two large eggs, lightly beaten
- 1 3/4 cups warm water
- Three tablespoons canola oil
- 1 cup brown rice flour
- 3/4 cup oat flour
- 1/4 cup tapioca starch
- 1 1/4 cups potato starch
- 1 1/2 teaspoons salt
- Two tablespoons brown sugar
- Two tablespoons gluten-free flaxseed meal
- 1/2 cup nonfat dry milk powder
- 2 1/2 teaspoons xanthan gum
- Three tablespoons psyllium, whole husks
- 2 1/2 teaspoons gluten-free yeast for bread machines

DIRECTIONS

1. Add the eggs, water, and canola oil to the bread maker pan and stir until combined.
2. Whisk all of the dry ingredients except the yeast together in a large mixing bowl.
3. Add the dry ingredients on topmost of the wet ingredients.
4. Create a well in the center of the dry ingredients and add the yeast.
5. Set Gluten-Free cycle, medium crust color, and then press Start.
6. When the bread is done, lay the pan on its side to cool before slicing to serve.

NUTRITION

Calories: 201	Fat: 5.7 g
Sodium: 390 mg	Carbs: 35.5 g
Dietary Fiber: 10.6 g	Protein: 5.1 g

109. EASY GLUTEN-FREE, DAIRY-FREE BREAD

PREPARATION	COOKING	SERVES
15 MIN	2 HOURS 10 MIN	12

INGREDIENTS

- 1 1/2 cups warm water
- Two teaspoons active dry yeast
- Two teaspoons sugar
- Two eggs, room temperature
- One egg white, room temperature
- 1 1/2 tablespoons apple cider vinegar
- 4 1/2 tablespoons olive oil
- 3 1/3 cups multi-purpose gluten-free flour

DIRECTIONS

1. Start with adding the yeast and sugar to the water, then stir to mix in a large mixing bowl; set aside until foamy, about 8 to 10 minutes.
2. Whisk the two eggs and one egg white together in a separate mixing bowl and add to the bread maker's baking pan.
3. Pour apple cider vinegar and oil into baking pan.
4. Add foamy yeast/water mixture to baking pan.
5. Add the multi-purpose gluten-free flour on top.
6. Set for Gluten-Free bread setting and Start.
7. Remove and invert the pan onto a cooling rack to remove the bread from the baking pan. Allow cooling completely before slicing to serve.

NUTRITION

Calories: 241
Sodium: 164 mg
Dietary Fiber: 5.6 g

Fat: 6.8 g
Carbs: 41 g
Protein: 4.5 g

110. GLUTEN-FREE SOURDOUGH BREAD

PREPARATION	COOKING	SERVES
5 MIN	3 HOURS	12

INGREDIENTS

- 1 cup of water
- Three eggs
- 3/4 cup ricotta cheese
- 1/4 cup honey
- 1/4 cup vegetable oil
- One teaspoon cider vinegar
- 3/4 cup gluten-free sourdough starter

- 2 cups white rice flour
- 2/3 cup potato starch
- 1/3 cup tapioca flour
- 1/2 cup dry milk powder
- 3 1/2 teaspoons xanthan gum
- 1 1/2 teaspoons salt

DIRECTIONS

1. Combine wet ingredients and pour into bread maker pan.
2. Mix dry ingredients in a large mixing bowl, and add on top of the wet ingredients.
3. Select the Gluten-Free cycle and press Start.
4. Remove the pan from the machine and allow the bread to remain in the pan for approximately 10 minutes.
5. Transfer to a cooling rack before slicing.

NUTRITION

Calories: 299
Sodium: 327 mg
Dietary Fiber: 1.0 g

Fat: 7.3 g
Carbs: 46 g
Protein: 5.2 g

111. GLUTEN-FREE CRUSTY BOULE BREAD

PREPARATION	COOKING	SERVES
15 MIN	3 HOURS	12

INGREDIENTS

- 3 1/4 cups gluten-free flour mix
- One tablespoon active dry yeast
- 1 1/2 teaspoons kosher salt
- One tablespoon guar gum
- 1 1/3 cups warm water
- Two large eggs, room temperature
- Two tablespoons, plus two teaspoons olive oil
- One tablespoon honey

DIRECTIONS

1. Combine all of the dry ingredients, do not include the yeast, in a large mixing bowl; set aside.
2. Mix the water, eggs, oil, and honey in a separate mixing bowl.
3. Pour the wet ingredients into the bread maker.
4. I am adding the dry ingredients on top of the wet ingredients.
5. Form a well in the center part of the dry ingredients and add the yeast.
6. Set to Gluten-Free setting and press Start.
7. Remove baked bread and allow it to cool completely. Hollow out and fill with soup or dip to use as a boule or slice for serving.

NUTRITION

Calories: 480
Sodium: 490 mg
Dietary Fiber: 67.9 g

Fat: 3.2 g
Carbs: 103.9 g
Protein: 2.4 g

112. GLUTEN-FREE POTATO BREAD

PREPARATION	COOKING	SERVES
5 MIN	3 HOURS	12

INGREDIENTS

- One medium russet potato, baked, or mashed leftovers
- Two packets gluten-free quick yeast
- Three tablespoons honey
- 3/4 cup warm almond milk
- Two eggs, one egg white

- 3 2/3 cups almond flour
- 3/4 cup tapioca flour
- One teaspoon sea salt
- One teaspoon dried chive
- One tablespoon apple cider vinegar
- 1/4 cup olive oil

DIRECTIONS

1. Combine the entire dry ingredients, except the yeast, in a large mixing bowl; set aside.
2. Whisk together the milk, eggs, oil, apple cider, and honey in a separate mixing bowl.
3. Pour the wet ingredients into the bread maker.
4. Add the dry ingredients on top of the wet ingredients.
5. Produce a well in the dry ingredients and add the yeast.
6. Set to Gluten-Free bread setting, light crust color, and press Start.
7. Allow cooling completely before slicing.

NUTRITION

Calories: 232
Sodium: 173 mg
Dietary Fiber: 6.3 g

Fat: 13.2 g
Carbs: 17.4 g
Protein: 10.4 g

113. SORGHUM BREAD

PREPARATION	COOKING	SERVES
5 MIN	3 HOURS	12

INGREDIENTS

- 1 1/2 cups sorghum flour
- 1/2 cup tapioca starch
- 1/2 cup brown rice flour
- One teaspoon xanthan gum
- One teaspoon guar gum
- 1/3 teaspoon salt
- Three tablespoons sugar

- 2 1/4 teaspoons instant yeast
- Three eggs (room temperature, lightly beaten)
- 1/4 cup oil
- 1 1/2 teaspoons vinegar
- 3/4-1 cup milk (105 - 115°F)

DIRECTIONS

1. Blend the dry ingredients in a bowl, not including the yeast.
2. Add the wet ingredients to the bread maker pan, then add the dry ingredients on top.
3. Next is making a well in the center of the dry ingredients and add the yeast.
4. Set to Basic bread cycle, light crust color, and press Start.
5. Remove and lay on its side to cool on a wire rack before serving.

NUTRITION

Calories: 169
Sodium: 151 mg
Dietary Fiber: 2.5 g

Fat: 6.3 g
Carbs: 25.8 g
Protein: 3.3 g

114. PALEO BREAD

PREPARATION	COOKING	SERVES
10 MIN	3 HOURS 15 MIN	16

INGREDIENTS

- Four tablespoons chia seeds
- One tablespoon flax meal
- 3/4 cup, plus one tablespoon water
- 1/4 cup coconut oil
- Three eggs, room temperature
- 1/2 cup almond milk
- One tablespoon honey
- 2 cups almond flour
- 1 1/4 cups tapioca flour
- 1/3 cup coconut flour
- One teaspoon salt
- 1/4 cup flax meal
- Two teaspoons cream of tartar
- One teaspoon baking soda
- Two teaspoons active dry yeast

DIRECTIONS

1. Combine the chia seeds plus a tablespoon of flax meal in a mixing bowl; stir in the water, and set aside.
2. Dissolve the coconut oil in a dish, and let it cool down to lukewarm.
3. Whisk in the eggs, almond milk, and honey.
4. Whisk in the chia seeds and flax meal gel and pour it into the bread maker pan.
5. Stir the almond flour, tapioca flour, coconut flour, salt, and 1/4 cup of flax meal.
6. Whisk the cream of tartar and baking soda in a separate bowl and combine it with the other dry ingredients.
7. Put the dry ingredients into the bread machine.
8. Make a little well on top and add the yeast.
9. Start the machine on the Wheat cycle, light or medium crust color, and press Start.
10. Remove to cool completely before slicing to serve.

NUTRITION

Calories: 190
Sodium: 243 mg
Dietary Fiber: 5.2 g

Fat: 10.3 g
Carbs: 20.4 g
Protein: 4.5 g

115. GLUTEN-FREE OAT AND HONEY BREAD

PREPARATION	COOKING	SERVES
5 MIN	3 HOURS	12

INGREDIENTS

- 1 1/4 cups warm water
- Three tablespoons honey
- Two eggs
- Three tablespoons butter, melted
- 1 1/4 cups gluten-free oats
- 1 1/4 cups brown rice flour
- 1/2 cup potato starch
- Two teaspoons xanthan gum
- 1 1/2 teaspoons sugar
- 3/4 teaspoon salt
- 1 1/2 tablespoons active dry yeast

DIRECTIONS

1. Add ingredients in the order listed above, except for the yeast.
2. Then form a well in the center of the dry ingredients and add the yeast.
3. Select the Gluten-Free cycle, light crust color, and press Start.
4. Remove bread and allow the bread to cool on its side on a cooling rack for 20 minutes before slicing to serve.

NUTRITION

Calories: 151
Sodium: 265 mg
Dietary Fiber: 4.3 g

Fat: 4.5 g
Carbs: 27.2 g
Protein: 3.5 g

116. GLUTEN-FREE CINNAMON RAISIN BREAD

PREPARATION	COOKING	SERVES
5 MIN	3 HOURS	12

INGREDIENTS

- 3/4 cup almond milk
- Two tablespoons flax meal
- Six tablespoons warm water
- 1 1/2 teaspoons apple cider vinegar
- Two tablespoons butter
- 1 1/2 tablespoons honey
- 1 2/3 cups brown rice flour
- 1/4 cup corn starch
- Two tablespoons potato starch
- 1 1/2 teaspoons xanthan gum
- One tablespoon cinnamon
- 1/2 teaspoon salt
- One teaspoon active dry yeast
- 1/2 cup raisins

DIRECTIONS

1. Mix flax and water and let the mixture stand for 5 minutes.
2. Combine dry ingredients in a separate bowl, except for the yeast.
3. Add wet ingredients to the bread machine.
4. Add the dry mixture on top and make a well in the middle of the dry mix.
5. Add the yeast to the well.
6. Set to Gluten-Free, light crust color, and press Start.
7. After the first kneading and rise cycle, add raisins.
8. Remove to a cooling rack when baked and let cool for 15 minutes before slicing.

NUTRITION

Calories: 192
Sodium: 173 mg
Dietary Fiber: 4.4 g

Fat: 4.7 g
Carbs: 38.2 g
Protein: 2.7 g

SOURDOUGH BREADS

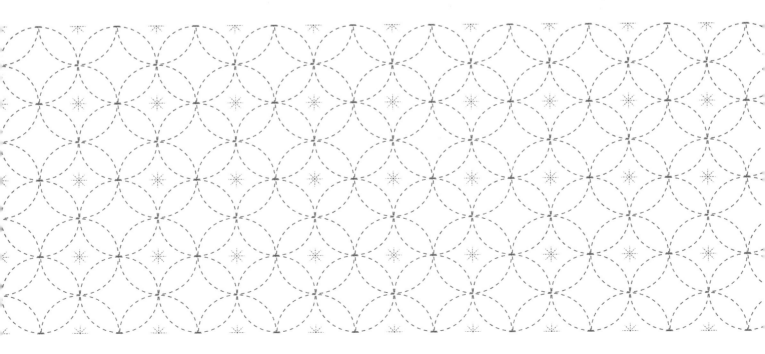

117. SOURDOUGH STARTER

PREPARATION	COOKING	SERVES	DIFFICULTY
5 MIN	–	–	BEGINNERS

INGREDIENTS

- cups warm water
- 1 tablespoon sugar
- 1 active dry yeast
- cups flour
- 1 proper container
- 1 spoon for stirring

DIRECTIONS

Day 1:

Combine the water, yeast, and sugar in a medium bowl, and whisk to combine. Gently stir in the flour until well combined, and transfer to your container. Let it sit, loosely covered, in a warm spot for 24 hours.

Day 2 – 4

Unlike the traditional starter, you don't need to feed this one yet. Stir it once or twice every 24 hours.

Day 5:

By now the starter should have developed the classic slightly sour smell. If not, don't worry; you just need to let it sit a bit longer. If it is ready, store it in the fridge, and feed it once a week until you're ready to use it. As with the traditional starter, you'll need to feed it the day before you plan to use it.

NUTRITION

Calories: 26 Cal
Fat: 0 g

Carbohydrates:6 g
Protein: 1 g

118. GARLIC AND HERB FLATBREAD SOURDOUGH

PREPARATION	COOKING	SERVES	DIFFICULTY
60 MIN	25-30 MIN	12	EXPERT

INGREDIENTS

- Dough
- 1 cup sourdough starter, fed or unfed
- 3/4 cup warm water
- teaspoons instant yeast
- cups all-purpose flour
- 1 1/2 teaspoons salt
- tablespoons olive oil
- Topping

- 1/2 teaspoon dried thyme
- 1/2 teaspoon dried oregano
- 1/2 teaspoon dried marjoram
- 1 teaspoon garlic powder
- 1/4 teaspoon onion powder
- 1/4 teaspoon salt
- 1/4 teaspoon pepper
- tablespoons olive oil

DIRECTIONS

1. Combine all the dough ingredients in the bowl of a stand mixer, and knead until smooth. Place in a lightly greased bowl and let rise for at least one hour. Punch down, then let rise again for at least one hour.
2. To prepare the topping, mix all ingredients except the olive oil in a small bowl.
3. Lightly grease a 9x13 baking pan or standard baking sheet, and pat and roll the dough into a long rectangle in the pan. Brush the olive oil over the dough, and sprinkle the herb and seasoning mixture over top. Cover and let rise for 15-20 minutes.
4. Preheat oven to 425F and bake for 25-30 minutes.

NUTRITION

Calories: 89 Cal
Fat: 3.7 g
Protein: 1.8 g

119. DINNER ROLLS

PREPARATION	COOKING	SERVES	DIFFICULTY
3 HOURS	5-10 MIN	24 ROLLS	EXPERT

INGREDIENTS

- 1 cup sourdough starter
- 1 1/2 cups warm water
- 1 tablespoon yeast
- 1 tablespoon salt
- tablespoons sugar
- tablespoons olive oil
- cups all-purpose flour
- tablespoons butter, melted

DIRECTIONS

1. In a large bowl, mix the sourdough starter, water, yeast, salt, sugar, and oil. Add the flour, stirring until the mixture forms a dough. If needed, add more flour. Place the dough in a greased bowl, and let it rise until doubled in size, about 2 hours.

2. Remove the dough from the bowl, and divide it into 2-3 inch sized pieces. Place the buns into a greased 9x13 pan, and let them rise, covered, for about an hour.

3. Preheat oven to 350F, and bake the rolls for 15 minutes. Remove from the oven, brush with the melted butter, and bake for an additional 5-10 minutes.

NUTRITION

Calories: 128 Cal
Fat: 2.4 g

Protein: 3.2 g
Sugar: 1.1 g

120. SOURDOUGH BOULE

PREPARATION	COOKING	SERVES	DIFFICULTY
4 HOURS	25-35 MIN	12	EXPERT

INGREDIENTS

- 275g Warm Water
- 500g sourdough starter
- 550g all-purpose flour
- 20g Salt

DIRECTIONS

1. Combine the flour, warm water, and starter, and let sit, covered for at least 30 minutes.
2. After letting it sit, stir in the salt, and turn the dough out onto a floured surface. It will be quite sticky, but that's okay. Flatten the dough slightly (it's best to "slap" it onto the counter), then fold it in half a few times.
3. Cover the dough and let it rise. Repeat the slap and fold a few more times. Now cover the dough and let it rise for 2-4 hours.
4. When the dough at least doubles in size, gently pull it so the top of the dough is taught. Repeat several times. Let it rise for 2-4 hours once more.
5. Preheat to oven to 475F, and either place a baking stone or a cast iron pan in the oven to preheat. Place the risen dough on the stone or pot, and score the top in several spots. Bake for 20 minutes, then lower the heat to 425F, and bake for 25-35 minutes more. The boule will be golden brown.

NUTRITION

Calories: 243 Cal
Fat: 0.7 g
Protein: 6.9 g

121. HERBED BAGUETTE

PREPARATION	COOKING	SERVES	DIFFICULTY
45 MIN	20-25 MIN	12	EXPERT

INGREDIENTS

- 1 1/4 cups warm water
- cups sourdough starter, either fed or unfed
- to 5 cups all-purpose flour
- 1/2 teaspoons salt
- teaspoons sugar
- 1 tablespoon instant yeast
- 1 tablespoon fresh oregano, chopped
- 1 teaspoon fresh rosemary, chopped
- 1 tablespoon fresh basil, chopped
- any other desired herbs

DIRECTIONS

1. In the bowl of a stand mixer, combine all ingredients, knead with a dough hook (or use your hands) until smooth dough forms -- about 7 to 10 minutes, if needed, add more flour.
2. Place the dough in an oiled bowl, cover, and allow to rise for about 2 hours.
3. Punch down the dough, and divide it into 3 pieces. Shape each piece of dough into a baguette -- about 16 inches long. You can do this by rolling the dough into a log, folding it, rolling it into a log, then folding it and rolling it again.
4. Place the rolled baguette dough onto lined baking sheets, and cover. Let rise for one hour.
5. Preheat oven to 425F, and bake for 20-25 minutes

NUTRITION

Calories: 197 Cal
Fat: 0.6 g
Protein: 5.8 g

122. PUMPERNICKEL BREAD

PREPARATION	COOKING	SERVES	DIFFICULTY
130 MIN	50 MIN	1 LOAF	EXPERT

INGREDIENTS

- 1 1/8 cups warm water
- 1 ½ tablespoons vegetable oil
- 1/3 cup molasses
- tablespoons cocoa
- 1 tablespoon caraway seed (optional)
- 1 ½ teaspoon salt

- 1 ½ cups of bread flour
- 1 cup of rye flour
- 1 cup whole wheat flour
- 1 ½ tablespoons of vital wheat gluten (optional)
- ½ teaspoon of bread machine yeast

DIRECTIONS

1. Add all ingredients to bread machine pan.
2. Choose basic bread cycle.
3. Take bread out to cool and enjoy!

NUTRITION

Calories: 97 Cal
Fat: 1 g

Carbohydrates:19 g
Protein: 3 g

123. SAUERKRAUT RYE

PREPARATION	COOKING	SERVES	DIFFICULTY
140 MIN	50 MIN	1 LOAF	EXPERT

INGREDIENTS

- 1 cup sauerkraut, rinsed and drained
- ¾ cup warm water
- 1½ tablespoons molasses
- 1½ tablespoons butter
- 1½ tablespoons brown sugar
- 1 teaspoon caraway seeds
- 1½ teaspoons salt
- 1 cup rye flour
- cups bread flour
- 1½ teaspoons active dry yeast

DIRECTIONS

1. Add all of the ingredients to your bread machine.
2. Set the program of your bread machine to Basic/White Bread and set crust type to Medium
3. Press START
4. Wait until the cycle completes
5. Once the loaf is ready, take the bucket out and let the loaf cool for 5 minutes
6. Gently shake the bucket to remove the loaf
7. Transfer to a cooling rack, slice and serve

NUTRITION

Calories: 74 Cal
Fat: 2 g
Carbohydrates:12 g

Protein: 2 g
Fiber: 1 g

124. CRUSTY SOURDOUGH BREAD

PREPARATION	COOKING	SERVES	DIFFICULTY
15 MINUTES ; 1 WEEK (STARTER)	3 HOURS	1 LOAF	EXPERT

INGREDIENTS

- 1/2 cup water
- cups bread flour
- tablespoons sugar

- 1 ½ teaspoon salt
- 1 teaspoon bread machine or quick active dry yeast

DIRECTIONS

1. Measure 1 cup of starter and remaining bread ingredients, add to bread machine pan.
2. Choose basic/white bread cycle with medium or light crust color.

NUTRITION

Calories: 165 calories;
Total Carbohydrate: 37 g
Total Fat: 0 g

Protein: 5 g
Sodium: 300 mg
Fiber: 1 g

125. HONEY SOURDOUGH BREAD

PREPARATION	COOKING	SERVES	DIFFICULTY
15 MINUTES ; 1 WEEK (STARTER)	3 HOURS	1 LOAF	BEGINNERS

INGREDIENTS

- 2/3 cup sourdough starter
- 1/2 cup water
- 1 tablespoon vegetable oil
- tablespoons honey
- 1/2 teaspoon salt
- 1/2 cup high protein wheat flour
- cups bread flour
- 1 teaspoon active dry yeast

DIRECTIONS

1. Measure 1 cup of starter and remaining bread ingredients, add to bread machine pan.
2. Choose basic/white bread cycle with medium or light crust color.

NUTRITION

Calories: 175 calories;
Total Carbohydrate: 33 g
Total Fat: 0.3 g

Protein: 5.6 g
Sodium: 121 mg
Fiber: 1.9 g

126. MULTIGRAIN SOURDOUGH BREAD

PREPARATION	COOKING	SERVES	DIFFICULTY
15 MINUTES ; 1 WEEK (STARTER)	3 HOURS	1 LOAF	BEGINNERS

INGREDIENTS

- cups sourdough starter
- tablespoons butter or 2 tablespoons olive oil
- 1/2 cup milk
- 1 teaspoon salt
- 1/4 cup honey

- 1/2 cup sunflower seeds
- 1/2 cup millet or 1/2 cup amaranth or 1/2 cup quinoa
- 1/2 cups multi-grain flour

DIRECTIONS

1. Add ingredients to bread machine pan.
2. Choose dough cycle.
3. Conventional Oven:
4. When cycle is complete, remove dough and place on lightly floured surface and shape into loaf.
5. Place in greased loaf pan, cover, and rise until bread is a couple inches above the edge.
6. Bake at 375 degrees for 40 to 50 minutes.

NUTRITION

Calories: 110 calories;
Total Carbohydrate: 13.5 g
Total Fat: 1.8 g

Protein: 2.7 g
Sodium: 213 mg
Fiber: 1.4 g

127. OLIVE AND GARLIC SOURDOUGH BREAD

PREPARATION	COOKING	SERVES	DIFFICULTY
15 MINUTES ; 1 WEEK (STARTER)	3 HOURS	1 LOAF	BEGINNERS

INGREDIENTS

- cups sourdough starter
- cups flour
- tablespoons olive oil
- tablespoons sugar
- teaspoon salt
- 1/2 cup chopped black olives
- cloves chopped garlic

DIRECTIONS

1. Add starter and bread ingredients to bread machine pan.
2. Choose dough cycle.
3. Conventional Oven:
4. Preheat oven to 350 degrees.
5. When cycle is complete, if dough is sticky add more flour.
6. Shape dough onto baking sheet or put into loaf pan
7. Bake for 35- 45 minutes until golden.
8. Cool before slicing.

NUTRITION

Calories: 150 calories;
Total Carbohydrate: 26.5 g
Total Fat: 0.5 g

Protein: 3.4 g
Sodium: 267 mg
Fiber: 1.1 g

128. CZECH SOURDOUGH BREAD

PREPARATION	COOKING	SERVES	DIFFICULTY
15 MINUTES ; 1 WEEK (STARTER)	3 HOURS	1 LOAF	BEGINNERS

INGREDIENTS

- 1 cup non-dairy milk
- 1 tablespoon salt
- 1 tablespoon honey
- 1 cup sourdough starter
- 1 1/2 cups rye flour
- 1 cup bread flour
- 3/4 cup wheat flour
- 1/2 cup grated half-baked potato
- tablespoons wheat gluten
- teaspoons caraway seeds

DIRECTIONS

1. Add ingredients to bread machine pan.
2. Choose the dough cycle.
3. The dough will need to rise, up to 24 hours, in the bread machine until doubles in size.
4. After rising, bake in bread machine for one hour.

NUTRITION

Calories: 198 calories;
Total Carbohydrate: 39.9 g
Total Fat: 0.8 g

Protein: 6.5 g
Sodium: 888 mg
Fiber: 4.3 g

129. FRENCH SOURDOUGH BREAD

PREPARATION	COOKING	SERVES	DIFFICULTY
15 MINUTES ; 1 WEEK (STARTER)	3 HOURS	2 LOAF	BEGINNERS

INGREDIENTS

- cups sourdough starter
- 1 teaspoon salt
- 1/2 cup water
- cups white bread flour
- tablespoons white cornmeal

DIRECTIONS

1. Add ingredients to bread machine pan, saving cornmeal for later.
2. Choose dough cycle.
3. Conventional Oven:
4. Preheat oven to 375 degrees.
5. At end of dough cycle, turn dough out onto a floured surface.
6. Add flour if dough is sticky.
7. Divide dough into 2 portions and flatten into an oval shape 1 ½ inch thick.
8. Fold ovals in half lengthwise and pinch seams to elongate.
9. Sprinkle cornmeal onto baking sheet and place the loaves seam side down.
10. Cover and let rise in until about doubled.
11. Place a shallow pan of hot water on the lower shelf of the oven;
12. Use a knife to make shallow, diagonal slashes in tops of loaves
13. Place the loaves in the oven and spray with fine water mister. Spray the oven walls as well.
14. Repeat spraying 3 times at one minute intervals.
15. Remove pan of water after 15 minutes of baking
16. Fully bake for 30 to 40 minutes or until golden brown.

NUTRITION

Calories: 937 calories;
Total Carbohydrate: 196 g
Total Fat: 0.4 g

Protein: 26.5 g
Sodium: 1172 mg
Fiber: 7.3 g

SPECIAL BREAD RECIPES

(holiday breads)

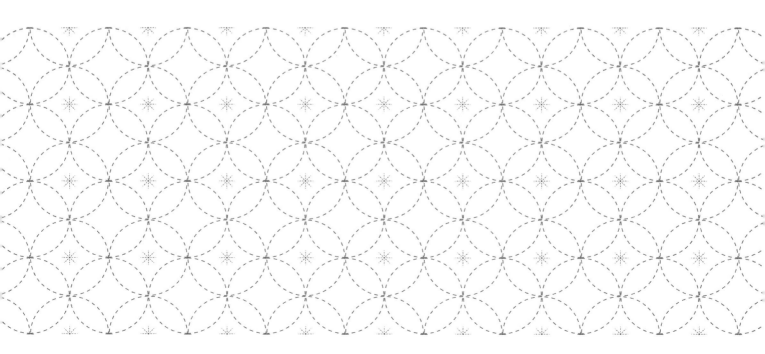

130. PUMPKIN BREAD

PREPARATION	COOKING	SERVES	DIFFICULTY
5 MIN	60 MIN	14	INTERMEDIATE

INGREDIENTS

- ½ cup plus 2 tablespoons warm water
- ½ cup canned pumpkin puree
- ¼ cup butter, softened
- ¼ cup non-fat dry milk powder
- 2¾ cups bread flour
- ¼ cup brown sugar
- ¾ teaspoon salt
- 1 teaspoon ground cinnamon
- ½ teaspoon ground ginger
- 1/8 teaspoon ground nutmeg
- 2¼ teaspoons active dry yeast

NUTRITION

Calories 134
Total Fat 3.6 g
Saturated Fat 2.1 g
Cholesterol 9 mg
Sodium 149 mg
Total Carbs 22.4 g
Fiber 1.1 g
Sugar 2.9 g
Protein 2.9 g

DIRECTIONS

1. Place all ingredients in the baking pan of the bread machine in the order recommended by the manufacturer.
2. Place the baking pan in the bread machine and close the lid.
3. Select Basic setting.
4. Press the start button.
5. Carefully, remove the baking pan from the machine and then invert the bread loaf onto a wire rack to cool completely before slicing.
6. With a sharp knife, cut bread loaf into desired-sized slices and serve.

131. PUMPKIN CRANBERRY BREAD

PREPARATION	COOKING	SERVES	DIFFICULTY
10 MIN	4 HOURS	12	INTERMEDIATE

INGREDIENTS

- ¾ cup water
- 2/3 cup canned pumpkin
- 3 tablespoons brown sugar
- 2 tablespoons vegetable oil
- 2 cups all-purpose flour
- 1 cup whole-wheat flour
- 1¼ teaspoon salt
- ½ cup sweetened dried cranberries
- ½ cup walnuts, chopped
- 1¾ teaspoons active dry yeast

NUTRITION

Calories 199
Total Fat 6 g
Saturated Fat 0.7 g
Cholesterol 0 mg
Sodium 247 mg
Total Carbs 31.4 g
Fiber 3.2 g
Sugar 5.1 g
Protein 5.6 g

DIRECTIONS

1. Place all ingredients in the baking pan of the bread machine in the order recommended by the manufacturer.
2. Place the baking pan in the bread machine and close the lid.
3. Select Basic setting.
4. Press the start button.
5. Carefully, remove the baking pan from the machine and then invert the bread loaf onto a wire rack to cool completely before slicing.
6. With a sharp knife, cut bread loaf into desired-sized slices and serve.

132. CRANBERRY BREAD

PREPARATION	COOKING	SERVES	DIFFICULTY
10 MIN	3 HOURS	16	INTERMEDIATE

INGREDIENTS

- 1 cup plus 3 tablespoons water
- ¼ cup honey
- 2 tablespoons butter, softened
- 4 cups bread flour
- 1 teaspoon salt
- 2 teaspoons bread machine yeast
- ¾ cup dried cranberries

NUTRITION

Calories 147
Total Fat 1.8 g
Saturated Fat 1 g
Cholesterol 4 mg
Sodium 159 mg
Total Carbs 28.97 g
Fiber 1.2 g
Sugar 4.6 g
Protein 3.5 g

DIRECTIONS

1. Place all ingredients (except the cranberries) in the baking pan of the bread machine in the order recommended by the manufacturer.
2. Place the baking pan in the bread machine and close the lid.
3. Select sweet bread setting.
4. Press the start button.
5. Wait for the bread machine to beep before adding the cranberries.
6. Carefully, remove the baking pan from the machine and then invert the bread loaf onto a wire rack to cool completely before slicing.
7. With a sharp knife, cut bread loaf into desired-sized slices and serve.

133. CRANBERRY ORANGE BREAD

PREPARATION	COOKING	SERVES	DIFFICULTY
10 MIN	3 HOURS	12	INTERMEDIATE

INGREDIENTS

- 3 cups all-purpose flour
- 1 cup dried cranberries
- ¾ cup plain yogurt
- ½ cup warm water
- 3 tablespoons honey
- 1 tablespoon butter, melted
- 2 teaspoons active dry yeast
- 1½ teaspoons salt
- 1 teaspoon orange oil

NUTRITION

Calories 166
Total Fat 2.7 g
Saturated Fat 1 g
Cholesterol 3 mg
Sodium 309 mg
Total Carbs 30.4 g
Fiber 1.3 g
Sugar 5.8 g
Protein 4.4 g

DIRECTIONS

1. Place all ingredients in the baking pan of the bread machine in the order recommended by the manufacturer.
2. Place the baking pan in the bread machine and close the lid.
3. Select Basic setting and then Light Crust.
4. Press the start button.
5. Carefully, remove the baking pan from the machine and then invert the bread loaf onto a wire rack to cool completely before slicing.
6. With a sharp knife, cut bread loaf into desired-sized slices and serve.

134. ORANGE BREAD

PREPARATION	COOKING	SERVES	DIFFICULTY
10 MIN	3 HOURS	12	INTERMEDIATE

INGREDIENTS

- 1¼ cups water
- 3 tablespoons powdered milk
- 1½ tablespoons vegetable oil
- 3 tablespoons honey
- 2½ cups bread flour
- ¾ cup amaranth flour
- 1/3 cup whole-wheat flour
- ¾ teaspoon salt
- 3 tablespoons fresh orange zest, grated finely
- 2¼ teaspoons active dry yeast

NUTRITION

Calories 197
Total Fat 2.9 g
Saturated Fat 0.6 g
Cholesterol 0 mg
Sodium 162 mg
Total Carbs 36.9 g
Fiber 2.6 g
Sugar 5.6 g
Protein 6.1 g

DIRECTIONS

1. Place all ingredients in the baking pan of the bread machine in the order recommended by the manufacturer.
2. Place the baking pan in the bread machine and close the lid.
3. Select Basic setting.
4. Press the start button.
5. Carefully, remove the baking pan from the machine and then invert the bread loaf onto a wire rack to cool completely before slicing.
6. With a sharp knife, cut bread loaf into desired-sized slices and serve.

135. BANANA CHOCOLATE CHIP BREAD

PREPARATION	COOKING	SERVES	DIFFICULTY
10 MIN	100 MIN	16	INTERMEDIATE

INGREDIENTS

- ½ cup warm milk
- 2 eggs
- ½ cup butter, melted
- 1 teaspoon vanilla extract
- 3 medium ripe bananas, peeled and mashed
- 1 cup granulated white sugar

- 2 cups all-purpose flour
- ½ teaspoon salt
- 2 teaspoons baking powder
- 1 teaspoon baking soda
- ½ cup chocolate chips

NUTRITION

Calories 215
Total Fat 8.2 g
Saturated Fat 5 g
Cholesterol 38 mg
Sodium 210 mg
Total Carbs 33.4 g
Fiber 1.2 g
Sugar 18.4 g
Protein 3.2 g

DIRECTIONS

1. Add ingredients (except for cranberries) in the baking pan of the bread machine in the order recommended by the manufacturer.
2. Place the baking pan in the bread machine and close the lid.
3. Select Quick Bread setting.
4. Press the start button.
5. Wait for the bread machine to beep before adding the chocolate chips.
6. Carefully, remove the baking pan from the machine and then invert the bread loaf onto a wire rack to cool completely before slicing.
7. With a sharp knife, cut bread loaf into desired-sized slices and serve.

136. SWEET POTATO BREAD

PREPARATION	COOKING	SERVES	DIFFICULTY
10 MIN	3 HOURS	16	INTERMEDIATE

INGREDIENTS

- ½ cup warm water
- 1 teaspoon pure vanilla extract
- 1 cup boiled sweet potato, peeled, and mashed
- 4 cups bread flour
- ½ teaspoon ground cinnamon

- 2 tablespoons butter, softened
- 1/3 cup brown sugar
- 1 teaspoon salt
- 2 teaspoons active dry yeast
- 2 tablespoons powdered milk

NUTRITION

Calories 155
Total Fat 1.8 g
Saturated Fat 1 g
Cholesterol 4 mg
Sodium 169 mg
Total Carbs 30.2 g
Fiber 1.4 g
Sugar 4.4 g
Protein 4.1 g

DIRECTIONS

1. Place all ingredients in the baking pan of the bread machine in the order recommended by the manufacturer.
2. Place the baking pan in the bread machine and close the lid.
3. Select White Bread setting.
4. Press the start button.
5. Carefully, remove the baking pan from the machine and then invert the bread loaf onto a wire rack to cool completely before slicing.
6. With a sharp knife, cut bread loaf into desired-sized slices and serve.

137. GINGERBREAD

PREPARATION	COOKING	SERVES	DIFFICULTY
10 MIN	3 HOURS	12	INTERMEDIATE

INGREDIENTS

- 3/4 cup milk
- 1/4 cup molasses
- 1 egg
- 3 tablespoons butter
- 3 1/3 cups bread flour
- 1 tablespoon brown sugar
- ¾ teaspoon salt
- ¾ teaspoon ground cinnamon
- ¾ teaspoon ground ginger
- 2¼ teaspoons active dry yeast
- 1/3 cup raisins

NUTRITION

Calories 202
Total Fat 4 g
Saturated Fat 2.2 g
Cholesterol 23 mg
Sodium 184 mg
Total Carbs 36.8 g
Fiber 1.3 g
Sugar 7.7 g
Protein 5 g

DIRECTIONS

1. Place all ingredients (except for raisins) in the baking pan of the bread machine in the order recommended by the manufacturer.
2. Place the baking pan in the bread machine and close the lid.
3. Select Basic setting and then Light Crust.
4. Press the start button.
5. Wait for the bread machine to beep before adding the raisins.
6. Carefully, remove the baking pan from the machine and then invert the bread loaf onto a wire rack to cool completely before slicing.
7. With a sharp knife, cut bread loaf into desired-sized slices and serve.

138. RAISIN CINNAMON SWIRL BREAD

PREPARATION	COOKING	SERVES	DIFFICULTY
15 MIN	3 HOURS 35 MIN	12	INTERMEDIATE

INGREDIENTS

Dough
- ¼ cup milk
- 1 large egg, beaten
- Water, as required
- ¼ cup butter, softened
- 1/3 cup white sugar
- 1 teaspoon salt
- 3½ cups bread flour

- 2 teaspoons active dry yeast
- ½ cup raisins

Cinnamon Swirl
- 1/3 cup white sugar
- 3 teaspoons ground cinnamon
- 2 egg whites, beaten
- 1/3 cup butter, melted and cooled

NUTRITION

Calories 297
Total Fat 10.6 g
Saturated Fat 6.3 g
Cholesterol 41 mg
Sodium 277 mg
Total Carbs 46.2 g
Fiber 1.7 g
Sugar 16.5 g
Protein 5.6 g

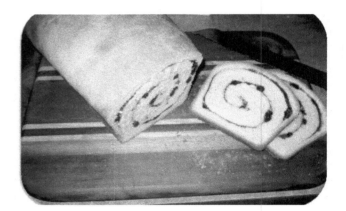

DIRECTIONS

1. For bread: Place milk and egg into a small bowl.
2. Add enough water to make 1 cup of mixture.
3. Place the egg mixture into the baking pan of the bread machine.
4. Place the remaining ingredients (except for raisins) on top in the order recommended by the manufacturer.
5. Place the baking pan in the bread machine and close the lid.
6. Select Dough cycle.
7. Press the start button.
8. Wait for the bread machine to beep before adding the raisins.
9. After Dough cycle completes, remove the dough from the bread pan and place onto lightly floured surface.
10. Roll the dough into a 10x12-inch rectangle.
11. For swirl: Mix together the sugar and cinnamon.
12. Brush the dough rectangle with 1 egg white, followed by the melted butter.
13. Now, sprinkle the dough with cinnamon sugar, leaving about a 1-inch border on each side.
14. From the short side, roll the dough and pinch the ends underneath.
15. Grease loaf pan and place the dough.
16. With a kitchen towel, cover the loaf pan and place in warm place for 1 hour or until doubled in size.
17. Preheat your oven to 350°F.
18. Brush the top of dough with remaining egg white.
19. Bake for approximately 35 minutes or until a wooden skewer inserted in the center comes out clean.
20. Remove the bread pan and place onto a wire rack to cool for about 15 minutes.
21. Cool bread before slicing

139. CHOCOLATE CHIP BREAD

PREPARATION	COOKING	SERVES	DIFFICULTY
10 MIN	2 HOURS 50 MIN	12	INTERMEDIATE

INGREDIENTS

- 1 cup milk
- ¼ cup water
- 1 egg, beaten
- 2 tablespoons butter, softened
- 3 cups bread flour
- 2 tablespoons white sugar
- 1 teaspoon salt
- 1 teaspoon ground cinnamon
- 1½ teaspoons active dry yeast
- ¾ cup semi-sweet mini chocolate chips

NUTRITION

Calories 226
Total Fat 7 g
Saturated Fat 4.1 g
Cholesterol 20 mg
Sodium 223 mg
Total Carbs 36.2 g
Fiber 1.8 g
Sugar 10 g
Protein 4.6 g

DIRECTIONS

1. Put ingredients (except the chocolate chips) in the baking pan of the bread machine in the order recommended by the manufacturer.
2. Place the baking pan in the bread machine and close the lid.
3. Select Mix Bread setting.
4. Press the start button.
5. Wait for the bread machine to beep before adding chocolate chips.
6. Carefully, remove the baking pan from the machine and then invert the bread loaf onto a wire rack to cool completely before slicing.
7. With a sharp knife, cut bread loaf into desired-sized slices and serve.

VEGETABLE BREADS

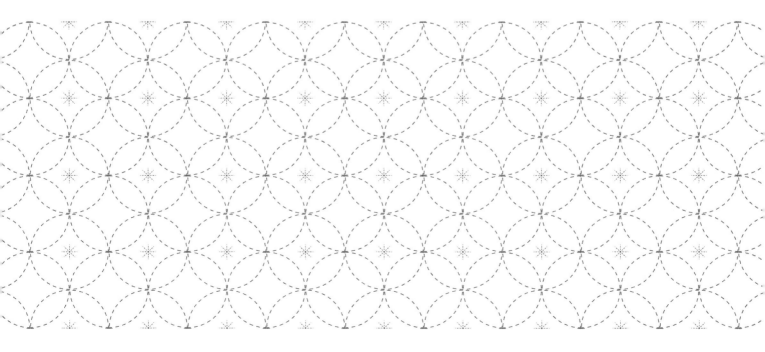

140. HEALTHY CELERY LOAF

PREPARATION	COOKING	SERVES	DIFFICULTY
2 HOURS 40 MIN	50 MIN	1 LOAF	EXPERT

INGREDIENTS

- 1 can (10 ounces) cream of celery soup
- tablespoons low-fat milk, heated
- 1 tablespoon vegetable oil
- 1¼ teaspoons celery salt
- ¾ cup celery, fresh/sliced thin
- 1 tablespoon celery leaves, fresh, chopped
- 1 whole egg
- ¼ teaspoon sugar
- cups bread flour
- ¼ teaspoon ginger
- ½ cup quick-cooking oats
- tablespoons gluten
- teaspoons celery seeds
- 1 pack of active dry yeast

DIRECTIONS

1. Add all of the ingredients to your bread machine, carefully following the instructions of the manufacturer
2. Set the program of your bread machine to Basic/White Bread and set crust type to Medium
3. Press START
4. Wait until the cycle completes
5. Once the loaf is ready, take the bucket out and let the loaf cool for 5 minutes
6. Gently shake the bucket to remove the loaf
7. Transfer to a cooling rack, slice and serve
8. Enjoy!

NUTRITION

Calories: 73 Cal
Fat: 4 g
Carbohydrates: 8 g

Protein: 3 g
Fiber: 1 g

141. BROCCOLI AND CAULIFLOWER BREAD

PREPARATION	COOKING	SERVES	DIFFICULTY
140 MIN	50 MIN	1 LOAF	EXPERT

INGREDIENTS

- ¼ cup water
- tablespoons olive oil
- 1 egg white
- 1 teaspoon lemon juice
- 2/3 cup grated cheddar cheese
- tablespoons green onion

- ½ cup broccoli, chopped
- ½ cup cauliflower, chopped
- ½ teaspoon lemon pepper seasoning
- cups bread flour
- 1 teaspoon bread machine yeast

DIRECTIONS

1. Add all of the ingredients to your bread machine, carefully following the instructions of the manufacturer
2. Set the program of your bread machine to Basic/White Bread and set crust type to Medium
3. Press START
4. Wait until the cycle completes
5. Once the loaf is ready, take the bucket out and let the loaf cool for 5 minutes
6. Gently shake the bucket to remove the loaf
7. Transfer to a cooling rack, slice and serve
8. Enjoy!

NUTRITION

Calories: 156 Cal
Fat: 8 g
Carbohydrates:17 g

Protein: 5 g
Fiber: 2 g

142. ZUCCHINI HERBED BREAD

PREPARATION	COOKING	SERVES	DIFFICULTY
140 MIN	50 MIN	1 LOAF	INTERMEDIATE

INGREDIENTS

- ½ cup water
- teaspoon honey
- 1 tablespoons oil
- ¾ cup zucchini, grated
- ¾ cup whole wheat flour
- cups bread flour
- 1 tablespoon fresh basil, chopped
- teaspoon sesame seeds
- 1 teaspoon salt
- 1½ teaspoon active dry yeast

DIRECTIONS

1. Add all of the ingredients to your bread machine, carefully following the instructions of the manufacturer
2. Set the program of your bread machine to Basic/White Bread and set crust type to Medium
3. Press START
4. Wait until the cycle completes
5. Once the loaf is ready, take the bucket out and let the loaf cool for 5 minutes
6. Gently shake the bucket to remove the loaf
7. Transfer to a cooling rack, slice and serve
8. Enjoy!

NUTRITION

Calories: 153 Cal
Fat: 1 g
Carbohydrates:28 g
Protein: 5 g
Fiber: 2 g

143. POTATO BREAD

PREPARATION	COOKING	SERVES	DIFFICULTY
3 HOURS	45 MIN	2 LOAVES	INTERMEDIATE

INGREDIENTS

- 1 3/4 teaspoon active dry yeast
- tablespoon dry milk
- 1/4 cup instant potato flakes
- tablespoon sugar
- cups bread flour
- 1 1/4 teaspoon salt
- tablespoon butter
- 1 3/8 cups water

DIRECTIONS

1. Put all the liquid ingredients in the pan. Add all the dry ingredients, except the yeast. Form a shallow hole in the middle of the dry ingredients and place the yeast.
2. Secure the pan in the machine and close the lid. Choose the basic setting and your desired color of the crust. Press starts.
3. Allow the bread to cool before slicing.

NUTRITION

Calories: 35calories;
Total Carbohydrate:
19 g
Total Fat: 0 g
Protein: 4 g

144. GOLDEN POTATO BREAD

PREPARATION	COOKING	SERVES	DIFFICULTY
2 HOURS 50 MIN	45 MIN	2 LOAVES	EXPERT

INGREDIENTS

- teaspoon bread machine yeast
- cups bread flour
- 1 1/2 teaspoon salt
- tablespoon potato starch
- 1 tablespoon dried chives
- tablespoon dry skim milk powder
- 1 teaspoon sugar
- tablespoon unsalted butter, cubed
- 3/4 cup mashed potatoes
- 1 large egg, at room temperature
- 3/4 cup potato cooking water, with a temperature of 80 to 90 degrees F (26 to 32 degrees C)

DIRECTIONS

1. Prepare the mashed potatoes. Peel the potatoes and put them in a saucepan. Pour enough cold water to cover them. Turn the heat to high and bring to a boil. Turn the heat to low and continue cooking the potatoes until tender. Transfer the cooked potatoes to a bowl and mash. Cover the bowl until the potatoes are ready to use. Reserve cooking water and cook until it reaches the needed temperature.
2. Put the ingredients in the bread pan in this order: potato cooking water, egg, mashed potatoes, butter, sugar, milk, chives, potato starch, salt, flour, and yeast.
3. Place the pan in the machine and close the lid. Turn it on. Choose the sweet setting and your preferred crust color. Start the cooking process.
4. Gently unmold the baked bread and leave to cool on a wire rack.
5. Slice and serve.

NUTRITION

Calories: 90calories;
Total Carbohydrate:
15 g
Total Fat: 2 g
Protein: 4 g
Protein: 4 g

145. ONION POTATO BREAD

PREPARATION	COOKING	SERVES	DIFFICULTY
80 MIN	45 MIN	2 LOAVES	INTERMEDIATE

INGREDIENTS

- tablespoon quick rise yeast
- cups bread flour
- 1 1/2 teaspoon seasoned salt
- tablespoon sugar
- 2/3 cup baked potatoes, mashed
- 1 1/2 cup onions, minced
- large eggs
- tablespoon oil
- 3/4 cup hot water, with the temperature of 115 to 125 degrees F (46 to 51 degrees C)

DIRECTIONS

1. Put the liquid ingredients in the pan. Add the dry ingredients, except the yeast. Form a shallow well in the middle using your hand and put the yeast.
2. Place the pan in the machine, close the lid and turn it on. Select the express bake 80 setting and start the machine.
3. Once the bread is cooked, leave on a wire rack for 20 minutes or until cooled.

NUTRITION

Calories: 160calories;
Total Carbohydrate:
44 g
Total Fat: 2 g
Protein: 6 g

146. SPINACH BREAD

PREPARATION	COOKING	SERVES	DIFFICULTY
140 MIN	40 MIN	1 LOAF	INTERMEDIATE

INGREDIENTS

- 1 cup water
- 1 tablespoon vegetable oil
- 1/2 cup frozen chopped spinach, thawed and drained
- cups all-purpose flour
- 1/2 cup shredded Cheddar cheese
- 1 teaspoon salt
- 1 tablespoon white sugar
- 1/2 teaspoon ground black pepper
- 1/2 teaspoons active dry yeast

DIRECTIONS

1. In the pan of bread machine, put all ingredients according to the suggested order of manufacture. Set white bread cycle.

NUTRITION

Calories: 121 calories;
Total Carbohydrate: 20.5 g
Cholesterol: 4 mg
Total Fat: 2.5 g
Protein: 4 g
Sodium: 184 mg

147. CURD BREAD

PREPARATION	COOKING	SERVES	DIFFICULTY
4 HOURS	15 MIN	12	INTERMEDIATE

INGREDIENTS

- ¾ cup lukewarm water
- 2/3 cups wheat bread machine flour
- ¾ cup cottage cheese
- Tablespoon softened butter
- Tablespoon white sugar
- 1½ teaspoon sea salt
- 1½ Tablespoon sesame seeds
- Tablespoon dried onions
- 1¼ teaspoon bread machine yeast

DIRECTIONS

1. Place all the dry and liquid ingredients in the pan and follow the instructions for your bread machine.
2. Pay particular attention to measuring the ingredients. Use a measuring cup, measuring spoon, and kitchen scales to do so.
3. Set the baking program to BASIC and the crust type to MEDIUM.
4. If the dough is too dense or too wet, adjust the amount of flour and liquid in the recipe.
5. When the program has ended, take the pan out of the bread machine and let cool for 5 minutes.
6. Shake the loaf out of the pan. If necessary, use a spatula.
7. Wrap the bread with a kitchen towel and set it aside for an hour. Otherwise, you can cool it on a wire rack.

NUTRITION

Calories: 277 calories;
Total Carbohydrate: 48.4 g
Cholesterol: 9 g
Total Fat: 4.7g

Protein: 9.4 g
Sodium: 547 mg
Sugar: 3.3 g

148. CURVY CARROT BREAD

PREPARATION	COOKING	SERVES	DIFFICULTY
120 MIN	15 MIN	12	INTERMEDIATE

INGREDIENTS

- ¾ cup milk, lukewarm
- tablespoons butter, melted at room temperature
- 1 tablespoon honey
- ¾ teaspoon ground nutmeg
- ½ teaspoon salt
- 1 ½ cups shredded carrot
- cups white bread flour
- ¼ teaspoons bread machine or active dry yeast

DIRECTIONS

1. Take 1 ½ pound size loaf pan and first add the liquid ingredients and then add the dry ingredients.
2. Place the loaf pan in the machine and close its top lid.
3. Plug the bread machine into power socket. For selecting a bread cycle, press "Quick Bread/ Rapid Bread" and for selecting a crust type, press "Light" or "Medium".
4. Start the machine and it will start preparing the bread.
5. After the bread loaf is completed, open the lid and take out the loaf pan.
6. Allow the pan to cool down for 10-15 minutes on a wire rack. Gently shake the pan and remove the bread loaf.
7. Make slices and serve.

NUTRITION

Calories: 142 calories;
Total Carbohydrate: 32.2 g
Cholesterol: 0 g
Total Fat: 0.8 g
Protein: 2.33 g

149. POTATO ROSEMARY BREAD

PREPARATION	COOKING	SERVES	DIFFICULTY
3 HOURS	30 MIN	20	INTERMEDIATE

INGREDIENTS

- cups bread flour, sifted
- 1 tablespoon white sugar
- 1 tablespoon sunflower oil
- 1½ teaspoons salt
- 1½ cups lukewarm water
- 1 teaspoon active dry yeast
- 1 cup potatoes, mashed
- teaspoons crushed rosemary

DIRECTIONS

1. Prepare all of the ingredients for your bread and measuring means (a cup, a spoon, kitchen scales).
2. Carefully measure the ingredients into the pan, except the potato and rosemary.
3. Place all of the ingredients into the bread bucket in the right order, following the manual for your bread machine.
4. Close the cover.
5. Select the program of your bread machine to BREAD with FILLINGS and choose the crust color to MEDIUM.
6. Press START.
7. After the signal, put the mashed potato and rosemary to the dough.
8. Wait until the program completes.
9. When done, take the bucket out and let it cool for 5-10 minutes.
10. Shake the loaf from the pan and let cool for 30 minutes on a cooling rack.
11. Slice, serve and enjoy the taste of fragrant homemade bread.

NUTRITION

Calories: 106 calories;
Total Carbohydrate: 21 g
Total Fat: 1 g
Protein: 2.9 g

Sodium: 641 mg
Fiber: 1 g
Sugar: 0.8 g

150. BEETROOT PRUNE BREAD

PREPARATION	COOKING	SERVES	DIFFICULTY
3 HOURS	30 MIN	20	INTERMEDIATE

INGREDIENTS

- 1½ cups lukewarm beet broth
- 5¼ cups all-purpose flour
- 1 cup beet puree
- 1 cup prunes, chopped
- tablespoons extra virgin olive oil
- tablespoons dry cream
- 1 tablespoon brown sugar
- teaspoons active dry yeast
- 1 tablespoon whole milk
- teaspoons sea salt

DIRECTIONS

1. Prepare all of the ingredients for your bread and measuring means (a cup, a spoon, kitchen scales).
2. Carefully measure the ingredients into the pan, except the prunes.
3. Place all of the ingredients into the bread bucket in the right order, following the manual for your bread machine.
4. Close the cover.
5. Select the program of your bread machine to BASIC and choose the crust color to MEDIUM.
6. Press START.
7. After the signal, put the prunes to the dough.
8. Wait until the program completes.
9. When done, take the bucket out and let it cool for 5-10 minutes.
10. Shake the loaf from the pan and let cool for 30 minutes on a cooling rack.
11. Slice, serve and enjoy the taste of fragrant homemade bread.

NUTRITION

Calories: 443 calories;
Total Carbohydrate: 81.1 g
Total Fat: 8.2 g
Protein: 9.9 g

Sodium: 604 mg
Fiber: 4.4 g
Sugar: 11.7 g

151. SUN VEGETABLE BREAD

PREPARATION	COOKING	SERVES
15 MIN	3 HOURS 45 MIN	8 SLICES

INGREDIENTS

- 2 cups (250 g) wheat flour
- 2 cups (250 g) whole-wheat flour
- 2 teaspoons panifarin
- 2 teaspoons yeast
- 1½ teaspoons salt
- 1 tablespoon sugar

- 1 tablespoon paprika dried slices
- 2 tablespoons dried beets
- 1 tablespoon dried garlic
- 1½ cups water
- 1 tablespoon vegetable oil

NUTRITION

Calories 253;
Total Fat 2.6g;
Saturated Fat 0.5g;
Cholesterol 0g;
Sodium 444mg;
Total Carbohydrate 49.6g;
Dietary Fiber 2.6g;
Total Sugars 0.6g;
Protein 7.2g

DIRECTIONS

1. Set baking program, which should be 4 hours; crust color is Medium.
2. Be sure to look at the kneading phase of the dough, to get a smooth and soft bun.

152. TOMATO ONION BREAD

PREPARATION	COOKING	SERVES
10 MIN	3 HOURS 50 MIN	12 SLICES

INGREDIENTS

- 2 cups all-purpose flour
- 1 cup whole meal flour
- ½ cup warm water
- 4 3/4 ounces (140 ml) milk
- 3 tablespoons olive oil
- 2 tablespoons sugar
- 1 teaspoon salt
- 2 teaspoons dry yeast
- ½ teaspoon baking powder
- 5 sun-dried tomatoes
- 1 onion
- ¼ teaspoon black pepper

NUTRITION

Calories 241;
Total Fat 6.4g;
Saturated Fat 1.1g;
Cholesterol 1g;
Sodium 305mg;
Total Carbohydrate 40g;
Dietary Fiber 3.5g;
Total Sugars 6.8g;
Protein 6.7g

DIRECTIONS

1. Prepare all the necessary products. Finely chop the onion and sauté in a frying pan. Cut up the sun-dried tomatoes (10 halves).
2. Pour all liquid ingredients into the bowl; then cover with flour and put in the tomatoes and onions. Pour in the yeast and baking powder, without touching the liquid.
3. Select the baking mode and start. You can choose the Bread with Additives program, and then the bread maker will knead the dough at low speeds.

153. TOMATO BREAD

PREPARATION	COOKING	SERVES
5 MIN	3 HOURS 30 MIN	8 SLICES

INGREDIENTS

- 3 tablespoons tomato paste
- 1½ cups (340 ml) water
- 4 1/3 cups (560 g) flour
- 1½ tablespoon vegetable oil
- 2 teaspoons sugar

- 2 teaspoons salt
- 1 ½ teaspoons dry yeast
- ½ teaspoon oregano, dried
- ½ teaspoon ground sweet paprika

NUTRITION

Calories 281;
Total Fat 3.3g;
Saturated Fat 0.6g;
Cholesterol 0g;
Sodium 590mg;
Total Carbohydrate 54.3g;
Dietary Fiber 2.4g;
Total Sugars 1.9g;
Protein 7.6g

DIRECTIONS

1. Dilute the tomato paste in warm water. If you do not like the tomato flavor, reduce the amount of tomato paste, but putting less than 1 tablespoon does not make sense, because the color will fade.
2. Prepare the spices. I added a little more oregano as well as Provencal herbs to the oregano and paprika (this bread also begs for spices).
3. Sieve the flour to enrich it with oxygen. Add the spices to the flour and mix well.
4. Pour the vegetable oil into the bread maker container. Add the tomato/water mixture, sugar, salt, and then the flour with spices, and then the yeast.
5. Turn on the bread maker (the Basic program — I have the WHITE BREAD — the crust Medium).
6. After the end of the baking cycle, turn off the bread maker. Remove the bread container and take out the hot bread. Place it on the grate for cooling for 1 hour.

154. CURD ONION BREAD WITH SESAME SEEDS

PREPARATION	COOKING	SERVES
10 MIN	3 HOURS 50 MIN	8 SLICES

INGREDIENTS

- 3/4 cup water
- 3 2/3 cups wheat flour
- 3/4 cup cottage cheese
- 2 tablespoons softened butter
- 2 tablespoon sugar

- 1 ½ teaspoons salt
- 1 ½ tablespoon sesame seeds
- 2 tablespoons dried onions
- 1 ¼ teaspoons dry yeast

NUTRITION

Calories 277;
Total Fat 4.7g;
Saturated Fat 2.3g;
Cholesterol 9g;
Sodium 547mg;
Total Carbohydrate 48.4g;
Dietary Fiber 1.9g;
Total Sugars 3.3g;
Protein 9.4g

DIRECTIONS

1. Put the products in the bread maker according to its instructions. I have this order, presented with the ingredients.
2. Bake on the BASIC program.

155. SQUASH CARROT BREAD

PREPARATION	COOKING	SERVES
15 MIN	3 HOURS 45 MIN	8 SLICES

INGREDIENTS

- 1 small zucchini
- 1 baby carrot
- 1 cup whey
- 1 ½ cups (180 g) white wheat flour
- 3/4 cup (100 g) whole wheat flour
- 3/4 cup (100 g) rye flour
- 2 tablespoons vegetable oil
- 1 teaspoon yeast, fresh
- 1 teaspoon salt
- ½ teaspoon sugar

NUTRITION

Calories 220;
Total Fat 4.3g;
Saturated Fat 0.8g;
Cholesterol 0g;
Sodium 313mg;
Total Carbohydrate 39.1g;
Dietary Fiber 4.1g;
Total Sugars 2.7g;
Protein 6.6g

DIRECTIONS

1. Cut/dice carrots and zucchini to about 8-10 mm (1/2 inch) in size.
2. In a frying pan, warm the vegetable oil and fry the vegetables over medium heat until soft. If desired, season the vegetables with salt and pepper.
3. Transfer the vegetables to a flat plate so that they cool down more quickly. While still hot, they cannot be added to the dough.
4. Now dissolve the yeast in the serum.
5. Send all kinds of flour, serum with yeast, as well as salt and sugar to the bakery.
6. Knead the dough in the Dough for the Rolls program.
7. At the very end of the batch, add the vegetables to the dough.
8. After adding vegetables, the dough will become moister. After fermentation process, which will last about an hour before the doubling of the volume of the dough, shift it onto a thickly floured surface.
9. Turn into a loaf and put it in an oiled form.
10. Conceal the form using a food film and leave for 1 to 1 1/3 hours.
11. Preheat oven to 450°F and put bread in it.
12. Bake the bread for 15 minutes, and then gently remove it from the mold. Lay it on the grate and bake for 15-20 minutes more

156. ZUCCHINI AND BERRIES LOAF

PREPARATION	COOKING	SERVES
60 MIN	25 MIN	8

INGREDIENTS

- 2 1/4 cups flour
- Three eggs whisked lightly
- 1 2/3 cups sugar
- 2 tsp. vanilla
- 3/4 cup vegetable oil
- 3/4 tsp. baking powder
- pinch of baking soda
- 1/4 tsp. salt
- 2 tsp. cinnamon
- 1 1/2 cup blueberries
- 1 1/2 cup shredded zucchini

DIRECTIONS

1. Preparing the Ingredients. Blend the dry and wet ingredients in two different bowls.
2. Place all ingredients, except the berries, in the bread pan in the liquid-dry-yeast-zucchini layering.
3. Put the pan in the Hamilton Beach bread machine.
4. Load the berries in the automatic dispenser.
5. Select the Bake cycle. Set to Rapid White bake for 1 hour. Press Start.
6. Five minutes into the cycle, add the berries.
7. Wait until the loaf is cooked.
8. The machine will start the keep warm mode after the bread is complete.
9. Let it stay in that mode for 10 minutes before unplugging.
10. Remove the pan and let it cool down for about 10 minutes.

NUTRITION

Calories 277
Cholesterol 9g
Carbohydrate 48.4g
Dietary Fiber 1.9g
Sugars 3.3g
Protein 9.4g

157. YEASTED CARROT BREAD

PREPARATION	COOKING	SERVES
10 MIN	25 MIN	8

INGREDIENTS

- ¾ cup milk
- Three tablespoons melted butter, cooled
- One tablespoon honey
- 1½ cups shredded carrot
- ¾ teaspoon ground nutmeg
- ½ teaspoon salt
- 3 cups white bread flour
- 2¼ teaspoons of dry yeast

DIRECTIONS

1. Preparing the Ingredients. Place the ingredients in your Hamilton Beach bread machine.
2. Select the Bake cycle. Program the machine for Rapid bread and press Start.
3. If the loaf is done, remove the bucket from the machine.
4. Let the loaf cool for 5 minutes.
5. Mildly shake the bucket to remove the loaf and try it out onto a rack to cool.

NUTRITION

Calories 277
Cholesterol 9g
Carbohydrate 48.4g
Dietary Fiber 1.9g
Sugars 3.3g
Protein 9.4g

158. ZUCCHINI RYE BREAD

PREPARATION	COOKING	SERVES
10 MIN	25 MIN	8

INGREDIENTS

- 2 cups all-purpose or bread flour
- 2 3/4 cup rye flour
- 2 tbsp. cocoa powder
- 1/2 cup cornmeal
- 1 tbsp. instant yeast
- 1/4 cup olive oil
- 3 tbsp. molasses or honey
- 1 1/2 cup lukewarm water
- 1 tsp. salt
- 1 1/2 cup zucchini, shredded

DIRECTIONS

1. Preparing the Ingredients. Dry the shredded zucchini but placing it in a towel and wringing it to remove excess moisture.
2. Place all the ingredients in the liquid-zucchini-flour-yeast layering.
3. Put the pan in the Hamilton Beach bread machine.
4. Select the Bake cycle. Choose White bread and medium crust.
5. Press start and wait until the loaf is cooked.
6. The machine will start the keep warm mode after the bread is complete.
7. Let it stay in that mode for nearly 10 minutes before unplugging.
8. Remove the pan and let it cool down for about 10 minutes

NUTRITION

Calories 277
Cholesterol 9g
Carbohydrate 48.4g
Dietary Fiber 1.9g
Sugars 3.3g
Protein 9.4g

159. SAVORY ONION BREAD

PREPARATION	COOKING	SERVES
10 MIN	25 MIN	8

INGREDIENTS

- 1 cup water, at 80°F to 90°F
- Three tablespoons melted butter, cooled
- 1 1/2 tablespoons sugar
- 11/8 teaspoons salt
- Three tablespoons dried minced onion
- 1 1/2 tablespoons chopped fresh chives
- 3 cups white bread flour
- One teaspoon bread machine or instant yeast

DIRECTIONS

1. Preparing the Ingredients. Place the ingredients in your Hamilton Beach bread machine.
2. Select the Bake cycle. Program the machine for Whitbread, pick the light or medium crust, and press Start.
3. Remove the bucket from the machine.
4. Let the loaf cool for 5 minutes.
5. Gently shake the bucket and turn it out onto a rack to cool.

NUTRITION

Calories 277
Cholesterol 9g
Carbohydrate 48.4g
Dietary Fiber 1.9g
Sugars 3.3g
Protein 9.4g

MEAT BREADS

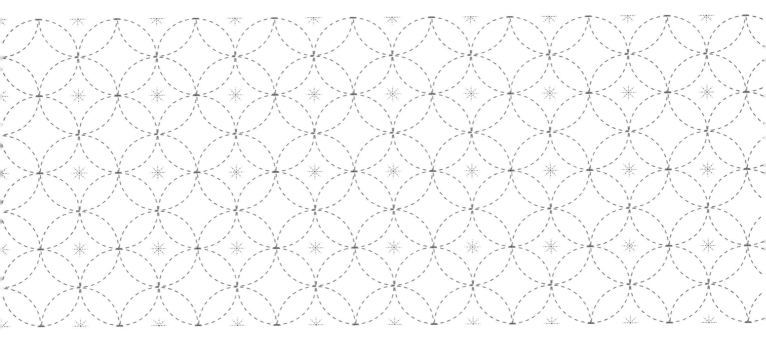

160. FRENCH HAM BREAD

PREPARATION	COOKING	SERVES
30-45 MIN	120 MIN	8

INGREDIENTS

- 3 1/3 cups wheat flour
- 1 cup ham
- ½ cup of milk powder
- 1 ½ tablespoons sugar
- One teaspoon yeast, fresh
- One teaspoon salt
- One teaspoon dried basil
- 1 1/3 cups water
- Two tablespoons olive oil

DIRECTIONS

1. Cut ham into cubes of 0.5-1 cm (approximately ¼ inch).
2. Put all ingredients in the bread maker from the following order: water, olive oil, salt, sugar, flour, milk powder, ham, and yeast.
3. Put all the ingredients according to the instructions in your bread maker.
4. Basil put in a dispenser or fill it later, at the signal in the container.
5. Turn on the bread maker.
6. After the end of the baking cycle, leave the bread container
7. In the bread maker to keep warm for 1 hour.
8. Then your delicious bread is ready!

NUTRITION

Calories 287
Total Fat 5.5g
Saturated Fat 1.1g
Cholesterol 11g
Sodium 557mg

Total Carbohydrate 47.2g
Dietary Fiber 1.7g
Total Sugars 6.4g
Protein 11.4g

161. MEAT BREAD

PREPARATION	COOKING	SERVES
90 MIN	90 MIN	8

INGREDIENTS

- 2 cups boiled chicken
- 1 cup milk 3 cups flour
- One tablespoon dry yeast one egg

- One teaspoon sugar
- ½ tablespoon salt
- Two tablespoons oil

DIRECTIONS

1. Pre-cook the meat. You can use a leg or fillet.
2. Separate meat from the bone and cut it into small pieces.
3. Pour all ingredients into the bread maker according to the instructions.
4. Add chicken pieces now.
5. The program is Basic.
6. This bread is perfectly combined with dill and butter.

NUTRITION

Calories 283
Total Fat 6.2g
Saturated Fat 1.4g
Cholesterol 50g
Sodium 484mg

Total Carbohydrate 38.4g
Dietary Fiber 1.6g
Total Sugars 2g
Protein 17.2g

162. ONION BACON BREAD

PREPARATION	COOKING	SERVES
90 MIN	90 MIN	8

INGREDIENTS

- 1 ½ cups water
- Two tablespoons sugar
- Three teaspoons dry yeast
- 4 ½ cups flour
- One egg
- Two teaspoons salt
- One tablespoon oil
- Three small onions, chopped
- 1 cup bacon

DIRECTIONS

1. Cut the bacon.
2. Put all ingredients into the machine.
3. Set it to the Basic program.
4. Enjoy this tasty bread!

NUTRITION

Calories 391
Total Fat 9.7g
Saturated Fat 2.7g
Cholesterol 38g
Sodium 960mg

Total Carbohydrate 59.9g
Dietary Fiber 2.8g
Total Sugars 4.3g
Protein 14.7g

163. FISH BELL PEPPER BRAN BREAD

PREPARATION	COOKING	SERVES
90 MIN	90 MIN	8

INGREDIENTS

- Ingredients
- 2 ½ cups flour
- ½ cup bran
- 1 1/3 cups water
- 1 ½ teaspoons salt
- 1 ½ teaspoons sugar
- 1 ½ tablespoon mustard oil
- One ¼ teaspoons dry yeast
- Two teaspoons powdered milk
- 1 cup chopped bell pepper
- ¾ cup chopped smoked fish
- One onion

DIRECTIONS

1. Grind onion and fry until golden brown.
2. Cut the fish into small pieces and the pepper into cubes.
3. Load all the ingredients in the bucket.
4. Turn on the baking program.
5. Bon Appetit!

NUTRITION

Calories 208
Total Fat 3.8g
Saturated Fat 0.5g
Cholesterol 8g
Sodium 487mg

Total Carbohydrate 35.9g
Dietary Fiber 4.2g
Total Sugars 2.7g
Protein 7.2g

164. SAUSAGE BREAD

PREPARATION	COOKING	SERVES
120 MIN	120 MIN	8

INGREDIENTS

- 1 ½ teaspoons dry yeast
- 3 cups flour
- One teaspoon sugar
- 1 ½ teaspoons salt
- 1 1/3 cups whey
- One tablespoon oil
- 1 cup chopped smoked sausage

DIRECTIONS

1. Fold all the ingredients in the order that is recommended specifically for your model.
2. Set the required parameters for baking bread.
3. When ready, remove the delicious hot bread.
4. Wait until it cools down and enjoy sausage.

NUTRITION

Calories 234
Total Fat 5.1g
Saturated Fat 1.2g
Cholesterol 9g
Sodium 535mg

Total Carbohydrate 38.7g
Dietary Fiber 1.4g
Total Sugars 2.7g
Protein 7.4g

165. CHEESE SAUSAGE BREAD

PREPARATION	COOKING	SERVES
120 MIN	120 MIN	8

INGREDIENTS

- One teaspoon dry yeast
- 3 ½ cups flour
- One teaspoon salt
- One tablespoon sugar
- 1 ½ tablespoon oil
- Two tablespoons smoked sausage
- Two tablespoons grated cheese
- One tablespoon chopped garlic
- 1 cup of water

DIRECTIONS

1. Cut the sausage into small cubes.
2. Grate the cheese on a grater
3. Chop the garlic.
4. Add all ingredients to the machine according to the instructions.
5. Turn on the baking program, and let it do the work.

NUTRITION

Calories 260
Total Fat 5.6g
Saturated Fat 1.4g
Cholesterol 8g
Sodium 355mg

Total Carbohydrate 43.8g
Dietary Fiber 1.6g
Total Sugars 1.7g
Protein 7.7g

166. CHEESY PIZZA DOUGH

PREPARATION	COOKING	SERVES
20 MIN	90 MIN	4

INGREDIENTS

- 1/2 cup warm beer, or more as needed
- 1 tbsp. Parmesan cheese
- 1 1/2 tsp. pizza dough yeast
- 1 tsp. salt
- 1 tsp. ground black pepper
- 1 tsp. granulated garlic
- 1 tbsp. olive oil
- 1 1/4 cups of all-purpose flour, or more if needed

DIRECTIONS

1. In a big mixing bowl, mix granulated garlic, pepper, salt, yeast, Parmesan cheese, and beer. Mix until salt dissolves. Allow mixture to stand for 10-20 minutes until yeast creates a creamy layer. Mix in olive oil.
2. Mix flour in yeast mixture until dough becomes smooth. Add small amounts of flour or beer if the dough is too sticky or dry. Let rise for an hour. Punch the dough and roll into a pizza crust on a work surface that's floured.

NUTRITION

Calories: 199
Total Carbohydrate: 32.4 g
Cholesterol: 1 mg

Total Fat: 4.2 g
Protein: 5.4 g
Sodium: 604 mg

167. COLLARDS & BACON GRILLED PIZZA

PREPARATION	COOKING	SERVES
15 MIN	15 MIN	4

INGREDIENTS

- 1 lb. whole-wheat pizza dough
- 3 tbsps. garlic-flavoured olive oil
- 2 cups thinly sliced cooked collard greens
- 1 cup shredded Cheddar cheese
- ¼ cup crumbled cooked bacon

DIRECTIONS

1. Heat grill to medium-high.
2. Roll out dough to an oval that's 12 inches on a surface that's lightly floured. Move to a big baking sheet that's lightly floured. Put Cheddar, collards, oil, and dough on the grill.
3. Grease grill rack. Move to grill the crust. Cover the lid and cook for 1-2 minutes until it becomes light brown and puffed. Use tongs to flip over the crust—spread oil on the crust and top with Cheddar and collards. Close lid and cook until cheese melts for another 2-3 minutes or the crust is light brown at the bottom.
4. Put pizza on the baking sheet and top using bacon.

NUTRITION

Calories: 498
Total Carbohydrate: 50 g
Cholesterol: 33 mg

Total Fat: 28 g Fiber: 6 g
Protein: 19 g Sodium: 573 mg
Sugar: 3 g Saturated Fat: 7 g

168. CRAZY CRUST PIZZA DOUGH

PREPARATION	COOKING	SERVES
10 MIN	45 MIN	8

INGREDIENTS

- 1 cup all-purpose flour
- 1 tsp. salt
- 1 tsp. dried oregano
- 1/8 tsp. black pepper
- Two eggs, lightly beaten
- 2/3 cup milk

DIRECTIONS

1. Heat the oven to 200 degrees C or 400 degrees F. Grease a baking sheet or rimmed pizza pan lightly.
2. Mix the black pepper, oregano, salt, and flour in a big bowl. Stir in milk and eggs thoroughly. Put butter in the pan and tilt it until it is evenly coated. Put whatever toppings you want on the top of the batter.
3. Bake it in the oven and set for 20-25 minutes until the crust is cooked
4. Take the crust out of the oven. Drizzle pizza sauce on and top with cheese. Bake for around 10 minutes until the cheese melts.

NUTRITION

Calories: 86
Total Carbohydrate: 13.1 g
Cholesterol: 48 mg

Total Fat: 1.8 g
Protein: 3.9 g
Sodium: 317 mg

169. DEEP DISH PIZZA DOUGH

PREPARATION	COOKING	SERVES
15 MIN	135 MIN	8

INGREDIENTS

- 1 (.25 oz.) package active dry yeast
- 1/3 cup white sugar
- 2/3 cup water
- 2 cups all-purpose flour
- 1 cup bread flour
- 1/4 cup corn oil
- 2 tsp. salt
- 6 tbsps. vegetable oil
- 1/2 cup all-purpose flour, or if it's needed

DIRECTIONS

1. Dissolve sugar and yeast in a bowl with water. Stand the mixture for 5 minutes until the yeast starts to form creamy foam and softens.
2. In a bowl, mix bread flour, salt, corn oil, and 2 cups of all-purpose flour. Add the yeast mixture. Knead the mixture in a work surface using 1/2 of the all-purpose flour until well-incorporated. Place the dough in a warm area, then rise for 2 hours until its size doubles.

NUTRITION

Calories: 328
Total Carbohydrate: 38.5 g
Cholesterol: 0 mg

Total Fat: 17.5 g Protein: 4.4 g
Sodium: 583 mg

170. DOUBLE CRUST STUFFED PIZZA

PREPARATION	COOKING	SERVES
30 MIN	2 HOURS 45 MIN	8

INGREDIENTS

- 1 1/2 tsp. white sugar
- 1 cup of warm water (100 degrees F or 40 degrees C)
- 1 1/2 tsp. active dry yeast
- 1 tbsp. olive oil
- 1/2 tsp. salt
- 2 cups all-purpose flour
- 1 (8 oz.) can crushed tomatoes
- 1 tbsp. packed brown sugar

- 1/2 tsp. garlic powder
- 1 tsp. olive oil
- 1/2 tsp. salt
- 3 cups shredded mozzarella cheese, divided
- 1/2 lb. bulk Italian sausage
- 1 (4 oz.) package sliced pepperoni
- 1 (8 oz.) package sliced fresh mushrooms
- 1/2 green bell pepper, chopped
- 1/2 red bell pepper, chopped

DIRECTIONS

1. In a large bowl or work bowl of a stand mixer, mix warm water and white sugar. Sprinkle with yeast and let the mixture stand for 5 minutes until the yeast starts to form creamy foam and softens. Stir in 1 tbsp. Of olive oil.
2. Mix flour with 1/2 tsp. of salt. Add half flour mixture into the yeast mixture and mix until no dry spots are visible. Whisk in remaining flour, a half cup at a time, mixing well every after addition. Put the dough on a lightly floured surface once it has pulled together. Knead the dough for 8 minutes until elastic and smooth. You can use the dough hook in a stand mixer to mix it.
3. Transfer it into a lightly oiled bowl and flip to coat the dough with oil. Use a light cloth to cover the dough. Rise it in a warm place for 1 hour until the volume doubles.
4. In a small saucepan, mix 1 tsp of olive oil, brown sugar, crushed tomatoes, garlic powder, and salt. Cover the saucepan and let it cook in low heat for 30 minutes until the tomatoes begin to break down.
5. Set the oven to 450°F for preheating. Flatten the dough and place it on a lightly floured surface. Divide the dough into two equal portions. Roll one part into a 12-inches thin circle, then Roll the other piece into a 9-inches thicker circle.
6. Press the the12-inches dough round into an ungreased 9-inches springform pan. Top the dough with a cup of cheese. Form sausage into a 9-inches patty and place it on top of the cheese. Arrange the pepperoni, green pepper, mushrooms, red pepper, and the remaining cheese on top of the sausage patty. Place the 9-inches dough around on the top, pinching its edges to seal. Make vent holes on the top of the crust by cutting several 1/2-inch. Pour the sauce evenly on the crust, leaving an only 1/2-inch border at the edges.
7. Bake the pizza inside the preheated oven for 40-45 minutes until the cheese is melted, then check sausage is cooked through when the crust is fixed. Let the pizza rest for 15 minutes. Before serving, cut the pizza into wedges.

NUTRITION

Calories: 410 Cal   Fat: 21.1 g
Carbohydrates: 32.5 g   Protein: 22.2 g

BREAKFAST BREADS

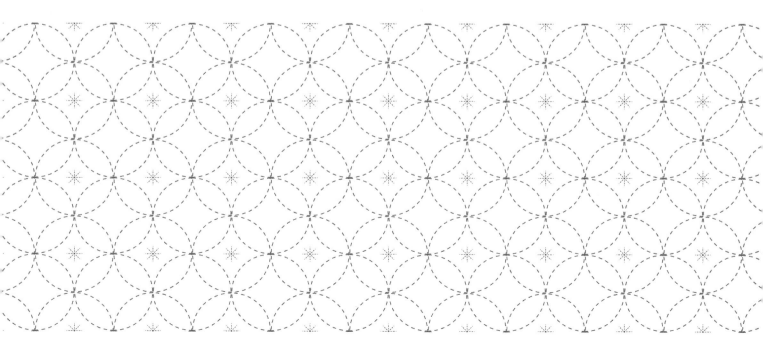

171. ENGLISH MUFFIN BREAD

PREPARATION	COOKING	SERVES
5 MIN	3 HOURS 40 MIN	14

INGREDIENTS

- 1 teaspoon vinegar
- 1/4 to 1/3 cup water
- 1 cup lukewarm milk
- 2 Tablespoon butter or 2 Tablespoon vegetable oil
- 1½ teaspoon salt
- 1½ teaspoon sugar
- ½ teaspoon baking powder
- 3½ cups unbleached all-purpose flour
- 2 1/4 teaspoon instant yeast

NUTRITION

Carbs: 13 g
Fat: 1 g
Protein: 2 g
Calories: 62

DIRECTIONS

1. Add each ingredient to the bread machine in the order and at the temperature recommended by your bread machine manufacturer.
2. Close the lid, select the basic bread, low crust setting on your bread machine, and press start.
3. When the bread machine has finished baking, remove the bread and put it on a cooling rack.

172. CRANBERRY ORANGE BREAKFAST BREAD

PREPARATION	COOKING	SERVES
5 MIN	3 HOURS 10 MIN	14

INGREDIENTS

- 1 1/8 cup orange juice
- 2 Tablespoon vegetable oil
- 2 Tablespoon honey
- 3 cups bread flour
- 1 Tablespoon dry milk powder
- ½ teaspoon ground cinnamon
- ½ teaspoon ground allspice
- 1 teaspoon salt
- 1 (.25 ounce) package active dry yeast
- 1 Tablespoon grated orange zest
- 1 cup sweetened dried cranberries
- 1/3 cup chopped walnuts

NUTRITION

Carbs: 29 g
Fat: 2 g
Protein: 9 g
Calories: 56

DIRECTIONS

1. Add each ingredient to the bread machine in the order and at the temperature recommended by your bread machine manufacturer.
2. Close the lid, select the basic bread, low crust setting on your bread machine, and press start.
3. Add the cranberries and chopped walnuts 5 to 10 minutes before last kneading cycle ends.
4. When the bread machine has finished baking, remove the bread and put it on a cooling rack.

173. BUTTERMILK HONEY BREAD

PREPARATION	COOKING	SERVES
5 MIN	3 HOURS 45 MIN	14

INGREDIENTS

- ½ cup water
- ¾ cup buttermilk
- ¼ cup honey
- 3 Tablespoon butter, softened and cut into pieces
- 3 cups bread flour
- 1½ teaspoon salt
- 2¼ teaspoon yeast (or 1 package)

NUTRITION

Carbs: 19 g
Fat: 1 g
Protein: 2 g
Calories: 92

DIRECTIONS

1. Add each ingredient to the bread machine in the order and at the temperature recommended by your bread machine manufacturer.
2. Close the lid, select the basic bread, medium crust setting on your bread machine and press start.
3. When the bread machine has finished baking, remove the bread and put it on a cooling rack.

174. WHOLE WHEAT BREAKFAST BREAD

PREPARATION	COOKING	SERVES
5 MIN	3 HOURS 45 MIN	14

INGREDIENTS

- 3 cups white whole wheat flour
- ½ teaspoon salt
- 1 cup water
- ½ cup coconut oil, liquified
- 4 Tablespoon honey
- 2½ teaspoon active dry yeast

NUTRITION

Carbs: 11 g
Fat: 3 g
Protein: 1 g
Calories: 60

DIRECTIONS

1. Add each ingredient to the bread machine in the order and at the temperature recommended by your bread machine manufacturer.
2. Close the lid, select the basic bread, medium crust setting on your bread machine and press start.
3. When the bread machine has finished baking, remove the bread and put it on a cooling rack.

175. CINNAMON-RAISIN BREAD

PREPARATION	COOKING	SERVES
5 MIN	3 HOURS	4

INGREDIENTS

- 1 cup water
- 2 Tablespoon butter, softened
- 3 cups Gold Medal Better for Bread flour
- 3 Tablespoon sugar
- 1½ teaspoon salt
- 1 teaspoon ground cinnamon
- 2½ teaspoon bread machine yeast
- ¾ cup raisins

NUTRITION

Carbs: 38 g
Fat: 2 g
Protein: 4 g
Calories: 180

DIRECTIONS

1. Add each ingredient except the raisins to the bread machine in the order and at the temperature recommended by your bread machine manufacturer.
2. Close the lid, select the sweet or basic bread, medium crust setting on your bread machine and press start.
3. Add raisins 10 minutes before the last kneading cycle ends.
4. When the bread machine has finished baking, remove the bread and put it on a cooling rack.

176. BUTTER BREAD ROLLS

PREPARATION	COOKING	SERVES
50 MIN	45 MIN	24 ROLLS

INGREDIENTS

- 1 cup warm milk
- 1/2 cup butter or 1/2 cup margarine, softened
- 1/4 cup sugar
- 2 eggs
- 1 1/2 teaspoons salt
- 4 cups bread flour
- 2 1/4 teaspoons active dry yeast

DIRECTIONS

1. In bread machine pan, put all ingredients in order suggested by manufacturer.
2. Select dough setting.
3. When cycle is completed, turn dough onto a lightly floured surface.
4. Divide dough into 24 portions.
5. Shape dough into balls.
6. Place in a greased 13 inch by 9-inch baking pan.
7. Cover and let rise in a warm place for 30-45 minutes.
8. Bake at 350 degrees for 13-16 minutes or until golden brown.

NUTRITION

Carbs: 38 g
Fat: 2 g
Protein: 4 g
Calories: 18

177. CRANBERRY & GOLDEN RAISIN BREAD

PREPARATION	COOKING	SERVES
5 MIN	3 HOURS	14

INGREDIENTS

- 1 1/3 cups water
- 4 Tablespoon sliced butter
- 3 cups flour
- 1 cup old fashioned oatmeal
- 1/3 cup brown sugar
- 1 teaspoon salt
- 4 Tablespoon dried cranberries
- 4 Tablespoon golden raisins
- 2 teaspoon bread machine yeast

DIRECTIONS

1. Add each ingredient except cranberries and golden raisins to the bread machine one by one, according to the manufacturer's instructions.
2. Close the lid, select the sweet or basic bread, medium crust setting on your bread machine and press start.
3. Add the cranberries and golden raisins 5 to 10 minutes before the last kneading cycle ends.
4. When the bread machine has finished baking, remove the bread and put it on a cooling rack.

NUTRITION

Carbs: 33 g
Fat: 3 g
Protein: 4 g
Calories: 175

178. BREAKFAST BREAD

PREPARATION	COOKING	SERVES
15 MIN	40 MIN	16 SLICES

INGREDIENTS

- ½ tsp. Xanthan gum
- ½ tsp. salt
- 2 Tbsp. coconut oil
- ½ cup butter, melted
- 1 tsp. baking powder
- 2 cups of almond flour
- Seven eggs

DIRECTIONS

1. Preheat the oven to 355F.
2. Beat eggs in a bowl on high for 2 minutes.
3. Add coconut oil and butter to the eggs and continue to beat.
4. Line a pan with baking paper and then pour the beaten eggs.
5. Pour in the rest of the ingredients and mix until it becomes thick.
6. Bake until a toothpick comes out dry. It takes 40 to 45 minutes.

NUTRITION

Calories: 234
Fat: 23g
Carb: 1g
Protein: 7g

179. PEANUT BUTTER AND JELLY BREAD

PREPARATION	COOKING	SERVES
120 MIN	70 MIN	1 LOAF

INGREDIENTS

- 1 1/2 tablespoons vegetable oil
- 1 cup of water
- ½ cup blackberry jelly
- ½ cup peanut butter
- One teaspoon salt
- One tablespoon white sugar
- 2 cups of bread flour
- 1 cup whole-wheat flour
- 1 1/2 teaspoons active dry yeast

DIRECTIONS

1. Put everything in your bread machine pan.
2. Select the basic setting.
3. Press the start button.
4. Take out the pan when done and set aside for 10 minutes.

NUTRITION

Calories: 153 Cal
Carbohydrates: 20 g
Fat: 9g,
Cholesterol: 0mg
Protein: 4g

Fiber: 2g
Sugar: 11g
Sodium: 244mg
Potassium: 120mg

180. LOW-CARB BAGEL

PREPARATION	COOKING	SERVES
15 MIN	25 MIN	12

INGREDIENTS

- 1 cup protein powder, unflavored
- 1/3 cup coconut flour
- 1 tsp. baking powder
- ½ tsp. sea salt
- ¼ cup ground flaxseed
- 1/3 cup sour cream
- 12 eggs

- Seasoning topping:
- 1 tsp. dried parsley
- 1 tsp. dried oregano
- 1 tsp. Dried minced onion
- ½ tsp. Garlic powder
- ½ tsp. Dried basil
- ½ tsp. sea salt

DIRECTIONS

1. Preheat the oven to 350F.
2. In a mixer, blend sour cream and eggs until well combined.
3. Whisk together the flaxseed, salt, baking powder, protein powder, and coconut flour in a bowl.
4. Mix the dry ingredients until it becomes wet ingredients. Make sure it is well blended.
5. Whisk the topping seasoning together in a small bowl. Set aside.
6. Grease 2 donut pans that can contain six donuts each.
7. Sprinkle pan with about 1 tsp. topping seasoning and evenly pour batter into each.
8. Sprinkle the top of each bagel evenly with the rest of the seasoning mixture.
9. Bake in the oven for 25 minutes, or until golden brown.

NUTRITION

Calories: 134
Fat: 6.8g
Carb: 4.2g
Protein: 12.1g

181. PURI BREAD

PREPARATION	COOKING	SERVES
10 MIN	5 MIN	6

INGREDIENTS

- 1 cup almond flour, sifted
- ½ cup of warm water
- 2 Tbsp. clarified butter
- 1 cup olive oil for frying
- Salt to taste

DIRECTIONS

1. Salt the water and add the flour.
2. Make some holes in the center of the dough and pour warm clarified butter.
3. Knead the dough and let stand for 15 minutes, covered.
4. Shape into six balls.
5. Flatten the balls into six thin rounds using a rolling pin.
6. Heat enough oil to cover a round frying pan completely.
7. Place a puri in it when hot.
8. Fry for 20 seconds on each side.
9. Place on a paper towel.
10. Repeat with the rest of the puri and serve.

NUTRITION

Calories: 106
Fat: 3g
Carb: 6g
Protein: 3g

182. HOT DOG BUNS

PREPARATION	COOKING	SERVES
10 MIN	50 MIN	10

INGREDIENTS

- One ¼ cups almond flour
- 5 tbsp. psyllium husk powder
- 1 tsp. sea salt
- 2 tsp. baking powder
- One ¼ cups boiling water
- 2 tsp. lemon juice
- Three egg whites

DIRECTIONS

1. Preheat the oven to 350F
2. In a bowl, put all dry ingredients and mix well.
3. Add boiling water, lemon juice, and egg whites into the dry mixture and whisk until combined.
4. Mold the dough into ten portions and roll into buns.
5. Transfer into the preheated oven and cook for 40 to 50 minutes on the lower oven rack.
6. Check for doneness and remove it.
7. Top with desired toppings and hot dogs.
8. Serve.

NUTRITION

Calories: 104
Fat: 8g
Carb: 1g
Protein: 4g

183. HEALTHY LOW CARB BREAD

PREPARATION	COOKING	SERVES
15 MIN	35 MIN	8

INGREDIENTS

- 2/3 cup coconut flour
- 2/3 cup coconut oil (softened not melted)
- Nine eggs
- 2 tsp. Cream of tartar
- ¾ tsp. xanthan gum
- 1 tsp. Baking soda
- ¼ tsp. salt

DIRECTIONS

1. Preheat the oven to 350F.
2. Grease a loaf pan with 1 to 2 tsp. Melted coconut oil and place it in the freezer to harden.
3. Add eggs into a bowl and mix for 2 minutes with a hand mixer.
4. Add coconut oil into the eggs and mix.
5. Add dry ingredients to a second bowl and whisk until mixed.
6. Put the dry ingredients into the egg mixture and mix on low speed with a hand mixer until dough is formed and the mixture is incorporated.
7. Add the dough into the prepared loaf pan, transfer into the preheated oven, and bake for 35 minutes.
8. Take out the bread pan from the oven.
9. Cool, slice, and serve.

NUTRITION

Calories: 229
Fat: 25.5g Carb: 6.5g
Protein: 8.5g

184. SPICY BREAD

PREPARATION	COOKING	SERVES
10 MIN	40 MIN	6

INGREDIENTS

- ½ cup coconut flour
- Six eggs
- Three large jalapenos, sliced
- 4 ounces' turkey bacon, sliced
- ½ cup ghee
- ¼ tsp. baking soda
- ¼ tsp. salt
- ¼ cup of water

DIRECTIONS

1. Preheat the oven to 400F.
2. Cut bacon and jalapenos on a baking tray and roast for 10 minutes.
3. Flip and bake for five more minutes.
4. Remove seeds from the jalapenos.
5. Place jalapenos and bacon slices in a food processor and blend until smooth.
6. In a bowl, add ghee, eggs, and ¼-cup water. Mix well.
7. Then add some coconut flour, baking soda, and salt. Stir to mix.
8. Add bacon and jalapeno mix.
9. Grease the loaf pan with ghee.
10. Pour batter into the loaf pan.
11. Bake for 40 minutes.
12. Enjoy.

NUTRITION

Calories: 240
Fat: 20g

185. FLUFFY PALEO BREAD

PREPARATION	COOKING	SERVES
10 MIN	40 MIN	15

INGREDIENTS

- One ¼ cup almond flour
- Five eggs
- 1 tsp. lemon juice
- 1/3 cup avocado oil
- One dash black pepper
- ½ tsp. sea salt
- 3 to 4 tbsp. tapioca flour
- 1 to 2 tsp. Poppyseed
- ¼ cup ground flaxseed
- ½ tsp. baking soda
- Top with:
- Poppy seeds
- Pumpkin seeds

DIRECTIONS

1. Preheat the oven to 350F.
2. Line a baking pan with parchment paper and set aside.
3. In a bowl, add eggs, avocado oil, and lemon juice and whisk until combined.
4. In another bowl, add tapioca flour, almond flour, baking soda, flaxseed, black pepper, and poppy seed. Mix.
5. Add the lemon juice mixture into the flour mixture and mix well.
6. Add the batter into the prepared loaf pan and top with extra pumpkin seeds and poppy seeds.
7. Cover loaf pan and transfer into the prepared oven, and bake for 20 minutes. Remove cover and bake until an inserted knife comes out clean after about 15 to 20 minutes.
8. Remove from oven and cool.
9. Slice and serve.

NUTRITION

Calories: 149 Cal
Fat: 12.9 g
Carbohydrates: 4.4 g

SWEET BREAD

(cake, chocolate)

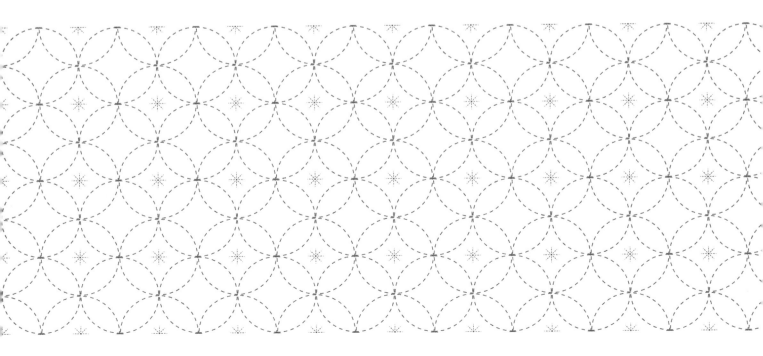

186. CHOCOLATE CHIP PEANUT BUTTER BANANA BREAD

PREPARATION	COOKING	SERVES
25 MIN	12 MIN	10-16 SLICES

INGREDIENTS

- Two bananas, mashed
- Two eggs, at room temperature
- 1/2 cup melted butter, cooled
- Two tablespoons milk, at room temperature
- One teaspoon pure vanilla extract
- cups all-purpose flour
- 1/2 cup sugar
- 11/4 teaspoons baking powder
- 1/2 teaspoon baking soda
- 1/2 teaspoon salt
- 1/2 cup peanut butter chips
- 1/2 cup semisweet chocolate chips

DIRECTIONS

1. Stir together the bananas, eggs, butter, milk, and vanilla in the bread machine bucket and set it aside.
2. In a medium bowl, toss together the flour, sugar, baking powder, baking soda, salt, peanut butter chips, and chocolate chips.
3. Add the dry ingredients to the bucket.
4. Program the machine for Quick/Rapid bread, and press Start.
5. When the cake is made, stick a knife into it, and if it arises out clean, the loaf is done.
6. If the loaf needs a few more minutes, look at the management panel for a Bake Only button, and extend the time by 10 minutes.
7. When the loaf is done, remove the bucket from the machine.
8. Let the loaf cool for 5 minutes.
9. Gently rock the can to remove the bread and turn it out onto a rack to cool.

NUTRITION

Calories: 297
Total Fat: 14g
Saturated Fat: 7g
Carbohydrates: 40g

Fiber: 1g
Sodium: 255mg
Protein: 4g

187. CHOCOLATE SOUR CREAM BREAD

PREPARATION	COOKING	SERVES
25 MIN	10 MIN	12

INGREDIENTS

- 1 cup sour cream
- Two eggs, at room temperature
- 1 cup of sugar
- 1/2 cup (1 stick) butter, at room temperature
- 1/4 cup plain Greek yogurt
- 13/4 cups all-purpose flour
- 1/2 cup unsweetened cocoa powder
- 1/2 teaspoon baking powder
- 1/2 teaspoon salt
- 1 cup milk chocolate chips

DIRECTIONS

1. In a small bowl, stick together the sour cream, eggs, sugar, butter, and yogurt until just combined.
2. Transfer the wet ingredients to the bread machine bucket, and then add the flour, cocoa powder, baking powder, salt, and chocolate chips.
3. Program the machine for Quick/Rapid bread, and press Start.
4. When the loaf is done, stick a knife into it, and if it comes out clean, the loaf is done.
5. If the loaf needs a few more minutes, check the control panel for a Bake Only button and extend the time by 10 minutes.
6. When the loaf is done, remove the bucket from the machine.
7. Let the loaf cool for 5 minutes.
8. Gently rock the can to remove the loaf and place it out onto a rack to cool.

NUTRITION

Calories: 347
Total Fat: 16g
Saturated Fat: 9g
Carbohydrates: 48g

Fiber: 2g
Sodium: 249mg
Protein: 6g

188. NECTARINE COBBLER BREAD

PREPARATION	COOKING	SERVES
10 MIN	5 MIN	12-16 SLICES

INGREDIENTS

- 1/2 cup (1 stick) butter, at room temperature
- Two eggs, at room temperature
- 1 cup of sugar
- 1/4 cup milk, at room temperature
- One teaspoon pure vanilla extract
- 1 cup diced nectarines
- 1 3/4 cups all-purpose flour
- One teaspoon baking soda
- 1/2 teaspoon salt
- 1/2 teaspoon ground nutmeg
- 1/4 teaspoon baking powder

DIRECTIONS

1. Place the butter, eggs, sugar, milk, vanilla, and nectarines in your bread machine.
2. Program the machine for Quick/Rapid bread and press Start.
3. While the wet ingredients are mixing, stir together the flour, baking soda, salt, nutmeg, and baking powder in a small bowl.
4. After the first fast mixing is done and the machine signals, add the dry ingredients.
5. When the loaf is done, remove the bucket from the machine.
6. Let the loaf cool for 5 minutes.
7. Gently shake the bucket to remove the loaf, then turn it out onto a rack to cool.

NUTRITION

Calories: 218
Total Fat: 9g
Saturated Fat: 5g
Carbohydrates: 32g

Fiber: 1g
Sodium: 270mg
Protein: 3g

189. SOUR CREAM MAPLE BREAD

PREPARATION	COOKING	SERVES
5 MIN	10 MIN	8

INGREDIENTS

- Six tablespoons water, at 80°F to 90°F
- Six tablespoons sour cream, at room temperature
- 1 1/2 tablespoons butter, at room temperature
- ¾ tablespoon maple syrup
- ½ teaspoon salt
- 1 3/4 cups white bread flour
- 1 1/6 teaspoons bread machine yeast

DIRECTIONS

1. Place the ingredients in your bread machine as recommended by the manufacturer.
2. Program the machine for Basic/White bread
3. Select light or medium crust, and then press Start.
4. When the loaf is done, remove the bucket from the machine.
5. Let the loaf cool for 5 minutes.
6. Gently shake the pan to get the loaf and turn it out onto a rack to cool.

NUTRITION

Calories: 149
Total Fat: 4g
Saturated Fat: 3g
Carbohydrates: 24g

Fiber: 1g
Sodium: 168mg
Protein: 4g

190. BARMBRACK BREAD

PREPARATION	COOKING	SERVES
10 MIN	25 MIN	8

INGREDIENTS

- 2/3 cup water
- One tablespoon melted butter cooled
- Two tablespoons sugar
- Two tablespoons skim milk powder
- One teaspoon salt
- One teaspoon dried lemon zest

- 1/4 teaspoon ground allspice
- 1/8 teaspoon ground nutmeg
- cups of white bread flour
- 1 1/2 teaspoons bread machine or active dry yeast
- 1/2 cup dried currants

DIRECTIONS

1. Place the ingredients, except the currants, in your bread machine as recommended by the manufacturer.
2. Program the system for Basic, select light or medium crust, and press Start.
3. Add the currants when your machine signals or when the second kneading cycle starts.
4. When the loaf is done, remove the bucket from the machine.
5. Let the loaf cool for 5 minutes.
6. Gently wobble the bucket to get the loaf and turn it out onto a rack to cool.

NUTRITION

Calories: 175
Total Fat: 2g
Saturated Fat: 1g
Carbohydrates: 35g

Fiber: 1g
Sodium: 313mg
Protein: 5g

191. APPLE BUTTER BREAD

PREPARATION	COOKING	SERVES
5 MIN	25 MIN	8

INGREDIENTS

- 2/3 cup milk
- 1/3 cup apple butter, at room temperature
- Four teaspoons melted butter, cooled
- Two teaspoons honey
- 2/3 teaspoon salt
- 2/3 cup whole-wheat flour
- 11/2 cups white bread flour
- One teaspoon instant yeast

DIRECTIONS

1. Place the ingredients in your bread machine as recommended by the manufacturer.
2. Program the system for Basic, choose light or medium crust, and press Start.
3. When the loaf is done, remove the bucket from the machine.
4. Let the loaf cool for 5 minutes.
5. Gently shake the bucket to remove the loaf and put it out onto a rack to cool.
6. Ingredient tip: Apple butter is simple to make in a slow cooker with very little fuss or mess. Making your own ensures you know what ingredients go into this tasty spread.

NUTRITION

Calories: 178
Total Fat: 3g
Saturated Fat: 2g
Carbohydrates: 34g

Fiber: 1g
Sodium: 220mg
Protein: 4g

192. CRUSTY HONEY BREAD

PREPARATION	COOKING	SERVES
5 MIN	25 MIN	8

INGREDIENTS

- 2/3 cup water
- One tablespoon honey
- 3/4 tablespoon melted butter, cooled
- 1/2 teaspoon salt
- 1 3/4 cups white bread flour
- One teaspoon instant yeast

DIRECTIONS

1. Place the ingredients in your bread machine as recommended by the manufacturer.
2. Program the vehicle for Basic/White bread, select light or medium crust, and press Start.
3. When the loaf is done, remove the bucket from the machine.
4. Let the loaf cool for 5 minutes.
5. Gently shake the bucket to remove the bread and turn it out onto a rack to cool.
6. Variation tip: Try adding semisweet chocolate chips and butterscotch chips for an unexpected twist on this simple bread. The resulting product will be gilded with the sweetness that gives the plain version a significant face-lift.

NUTRITION

Calories: 119
Total Fat: 1g
Saturated Fat: 1g
Carbohydrates: 24g

Fiber: 1g
Sodium: 155mg
Protein: 3g

193. HONEY GRANOLA BREAD

PREPARATION	COOKING	SERVES
5 MIN	25 MIN	8

INGREDIENTS

- 3/4 cups milk
- Two tablespoons honey
- One tablespoon butter, melted and cooled
- 3/4 teaspoons salt
- 1/2 cup whole-wheat flour
- 1/2 cup prepared granola, crushed
- 11/4 cups white bread flour
- One teaspoon instant yeast

DIRECTIONS

1. Place the ingredients in your bread machine as recommended by the manufacturer.
2. Program the system for Basic/White bread, select light or medium crust, and press Start.
3. When the loaf is done, remove the bucket from the machine.
4. Let the loaf cool for 5 minutes.
5. Gently shake the bucket to remove the loaf and place it out onto a rack to cool.
6. Ingredient tip: Choose granola with no dried fruit because you will be crushing it for this recipe. Dried fruit would create a lumpy mess in the dough, which would wreck the finished loaf texture.

NUTRITION

Calories: 151
Total Fat: 5g
Saturated Fat: 2g
Carbohydrates: 33g

Fiber: 2g
Sodium: 218mg
Protein: 6g

194. BLACK BREAD

PREPARATION	COOKING	SERVES
5 MIN	25 MIN	8

INGREDIENTS

- 1/2 cup water
- 1/4 cup brewed coffee, at 80°F to 90°F
- One tablespoon balsamic vinegar
- One tablespoon olive oil
- One tablespoon dark molasses
- 1/2 tablespoon light brown sugar
- 1/2 teaspoon salt
- One teaspoon caraway seed
- Two tablespoons unsweetened cocoa powder
- 1/2 cup dark rye flour
- 11/4 cups white bread flour
- One teaspoon instant yeast

DIRECTIONS

1. Place the ingredients in your bread machine as recommended by the manufacturer.
2. Program the machine for Whole-Wheat/Whole-Grain bread, select light or medium crust, and press Start.
3. When the loaf is done, remove the bucket from the machine.
4. Let the loaf cool for 5 minutes.
5. Gently shake the bucket to pick the loaf and turn it out onto a rack to cool.

NUTRITION

Calories: 123
Total Fat: 2g
Saturated Fat: 0g
Carbohydrates: 23g

Fiber: 3g
Sodium: 150mg
Protein: 4g

195. APPLE CIDER BREAD

PREPARATION	COOKING	SERVES
5 MIN	25 MIN	8

INGREDIENTS

- 1/4 cup milk
- Two tablespoons apple cider, at room temperature
- Two tablespoons sugar
- Four teaspoons melted butter, cooled
- One tablespoon honey
- 1/4 teaspoon salt
- cups white bread flour
- 3/4 teaspoons bread machine or instant yeast
- 2/3 apple, peeled, cored, and finely diced

DIRECTIONS

1. Place the ingredients, except the apple, in your bread machine as recommended by the manufacturer.
2. Program the machine for Basic/White bread, select light or medium crust, and press Start.
3. Add the apple when the machine signals or 5 minutes before the last kneading cycle is complete.
4. When the loaf is done, remove the bucket from the machine.
5. Let the loaf cool for 5 minutes.
6. Gently shake the bucket to remove the loaf and turn it out onto a rack to cool.
7. Ingredient tip: Look for apple cider sweetened and spiced well, so your bread rises nicely.

NUTRITION

Calories: 164
Total Fat: 3g
Saturated Fat: 1g
Carbohydrates: 31g

Fiber: 1g
Sodium: 70mg
Protein: 4g

196. BROWNIE BREAD

PREPARATION	COOKING	SERVES
75 MIN	50 MIN	1 LOAF

INGREDIENTS

- 1 egg
- 1 egg yolk
- 1 teaspoon Salt
- 1/2 cup boiling water
- 1/2 cup cocoa powder, unsweetened
- 1/2 cup warm water
- 1/2 teaspoon Active dry yeast
- tablespoon Vegetable oil
- teaspoon White sugar
- 2/3 cup white sugar
- cups bread flour

DIRECTIONS

1. Put the cocoa powder in a small bow. Pour boiling water and dissolve the cocoa powder.
2. Put the warm water, yeast and the 2 teaspoon White sugar in another bowl. Dissolve yeast and sugar. Let stand for about 10 minutes, or until the mix is creamy.
3. Place the cocoa mix, the yeast mix, the flour, the 2/3 cup white sugar, the salt, the vegetable, and the egg in the bread pan. Select basic bread cycle. Press starts.

NUTRITION

Calories: 70 Cal
Fat: 3 g

Carbohydrates: 10 g
Protein: 1 g

197. BLACK FOREST BREAD

PREPARATION	COOKING	SERVES
135 MIN	50 MIN	1 LOAF

INGREDIENTS

- 1 1/8 cups Warm water
- 1/3 cup Molasses
- 1 1/2 tablespoons Canola oil
- 1 1/2 cups Bread flour
- 1 cup Rye flour

- 1 cup Whole wheat flour
- 1 1/2 teaspoons Salt
- tablespoons Cocoa powder
- 1 1/2 tablespoons Caraway seeds
- teaspoons Active dry yeast

DIRECTIONS

1. Place all ingredients into your bread maker according to manufacture.
2. Select type to a light crust.
3. Press starts.
4. Remembering to check while starting to knead.
5. If mixture is too dry add tablespoon warm water at a time.
6. If mixture is too wet add flour again a little at a time.
7. Mixture should go into a ball form, and just soft and slightly sticky to the finger touch. This goes for all types of breads when kneading.

NUTRITION

Calories: 240 Cal
Fat: 4 g

Carbohydrates: 29 g
Protein: 22 g

198. SWEET ALMOND ANISE BREAD

PREPARATION	COOKING	SERVES
140 MIN	50 MIN	1 LOAF

INGREDIENTS

- ¾ cup water
- ¼ cup butter
- ¼ cup sugar
- ½ teaspoon salt
- cups bread flour
- 1 teaspoon anise seed
- teaspoons active dry yeast
- ½ cup almonds, chopped

DIRECTIONS

1. Add all of the ingredients to your bread machine, carefully following the instructions of the manufacturer
2. Set the program of your bread machine to Basic/White Bread and set crust type to Medium
3. Press START
4. Wait until the cycle completes
5. Once the loaf is ready, take the bucket out and let the loaf cool for 5 minutes
6. Gently shake the bucket to remove the loaf
7. Transfer to a cooling rack, slice and serve
8. Enjoy!

NUTRITION

Calories: 87 Cal
Fat: 4 g
Carbohydrates: 7 g

Protein: 3 g
Fiber: 1 g

199. CHOCOLATE GINGER AND HAZELNUT BREAD

PREPARATION	COOKING	SERVES
2 HOURS 50 MIN	45 MIN	2 LOAVES

INGREDIENTS

- 1/2 cup chopped hazelnuts
- teaspoon bread machine yeast
- 1/2 cups bread flour
- 1 teaspoon salt
- 1 1/2 tablespoon dry skim milk powder
- tablespoon light brown sugar

- tablespoon candied ginger, chopped
- 1/3 cup unsweetened coconut
- 1 1/2 tablespoon unsalted butter, cubed
- 1 cup, plus 2 tablespoon water, with a temperature of 80 to 90 degrees F (26 to 32 degrees C)

DIRECTIONS

1. Put all the ingredients, except the hazelnuts, in the pan in this order: water, butter, coconut, candied ginger, brown sugar, milk, salt, flour, and yeast.
2. Secure the pan in the machine and close the lid. Put the toasted hazelnuts in the fruit and nut dispenser.
3. Turn the machine on. Select the basic setting and your desired color of the crust and press start.
4. Once done, carefully transfer the baked bread to a wire rack until cooled.

NUTRITION

Calories: 273 calories;
Total Carbohydrate: 43 g
Total Fat: 11 g
Protein: 7 g

200. WHITE CHOCOLATE BREAD

PREPARATION	COOKING	SERVES
3 HOURS	15 MIN	12

INGREDIENTS

- 1/4 cup warm water
- 1 cup warm milk
- 1 egg
- 1/4 cup butter, softened
- cups bread flour
- tablespoons brown sugar
- tablespoons white sugar
- 1 teaspoon salt
- 1 teaspoon ground cinnamon
- 1 (.25 oz.) package active dry yeast
- 1 cup white chocolate chips

DIRECTIONS

1. Put all the ingredients together, except for the white chocolate chips, into the bread machine pan following the order suggested by the manufacturer.
2. Choose the cycle on the machine and press the Start button to run the machine.
3. Put in the white chocolate chips at the machine's signal if the machine used has a Fruit setting on it or you may put the white chocolate chips about 5 minutes before the kneading cycle ends.

NUTRITION

Calories: 277 calories;
Total Carbohydrate: 39 g
Cholesterol: 30 mg

Total Fat: 10.5 g
Protein: 6.6 g
Sodium: 253 mg

201. CINNAMON RAISIN BREAD

PREPARATION	COOKING	SERVES
5 MIN	3 HOURS	1 LOAF

INGREDIENTS

- 1 cup water
- tablespoons margarine
- cups flour
- tablespoons sugar

- 1 1/2 teaspoons salt
- 1 teaspoon cinnamon
- 1/2 teaspoons yeast
- 3/4 cup raisins

DIRECTIONS

1. Add all the ingredients into pan except raisins.
2. Choose sweet bread setting.
3. When the machine beeps, add in raisins.

NUTRITION

Calories: 141 calories;
Total Carbohydrate: 26 g
Cholesterol: 00 mg
Total Fat: 2 g

Protein: 3.5 g
Sodium: 329 mg
Fiber: 1 g

202. CHOCOLATE CHIP BREAD

PREPARATION	COOKING	SERVES
10 MIN	2 HOURS 50 MIN	1 LOAF

INGREDIENTS

- 1/4 cup water
- 1 cup milk
- 1 egg
- cups bread flour
- tablespoons brown sugar
- tablespoons white sugar

- 1 teaspoon salt
- 1 teaspoon ground cinnamon
- 1 1/2 teaspoon active dry yeast
- tablespoons margarine, softened
- 3/4 cup semisweet chocolate chips

DIRECTIONS

1. Add all the ingredients into pan except chocolate chips.
2. Choose mix bread
3. When the machine beeps, add in chips.

NUTRITION

Calories: 184 calories;
Total Carbohydrate: 30.6 g
Cholesterol: 14 mg
Total Fat: 5.2 g

Protein: 3.5 g
Sodium: 189 mg
Fiber: 1.3 g

203. PEANUT BUTTER BREAD

PREPARATION	COOKING	SERVES
10 MIN	3 HOURS	1 LOAF

INGREDIENTS

- 1 1/4 Cups water
- 1/2 cup Peanut butter – creamy or chunky
- 1 ½ cups whole wheat flour
- tablespoons Gluten flour
- 1 ½ cups bread flour
- 1/4 cup Brown sugar
- 1/2 teaspoon Salt –
- ¼ teaspoons Active dry yeast

DIRECTIONS

1. Add all the ingredients into pan.
2. Choose whole wheat bread setting, large loaf.

NUTRITION

Calories: 82 calories;
Total Carbohydrate: 13 g
Cholesterol: 13 mg
Total Fat: 2.2 g

Protein: 2.5 g
Sodium: 280 mg
Fiber: 1 g

204. HOT BUTTERED RUM BREAD

PREPARATION	COOKING	SERVES
10 MIN	3 HOURS 40 MIN	1 LOAF

INGREDIENTS

- 1 egg
- 1 tablespoon rum extract
- tablespoons butter, softened
- cups bread flour
- tablespoons packed brown sugar
- 1 ¼ teaspoon salt
- 1/2 teaspoon ground cinnamon
- 1/4 teaspoon ground nutmeg
- 1/4 teaspoon ground cardamom
- 1 teaspoon bread machine or quick active dry yeast

Topping:
- 1 egg yolk, beaten
- 1 ½ teaspoon finely chopped pecans
- 1 ½ teaspoon packed brown sugar

DIRECTIONS

1. Break egg into 1 cup, and add water to fil out measuring cup
2. Place egg mixture and bread ingredients into pan.
3. Choose basic bread setting and medium/light crust color.
4. While bread bakes, combine topping ingredients in small bowl, and brush on top of bread when there is 40 – 50 minutes remaining of the cook time.

NUTRITION

Calories: 170 calories;
Total Carbohydrate: 31 g
Cholesterol: 25 mg
Total Fat: 2.0 g

Protein: 4 g
Sodium: 270 mg
Fiber: 1 g

205. BUTTERY SWEET BREAD

PREPARATION	COOKING	SERVES
10 MIN	3 HOURS 40 MIN	1 LOAF

INGREDIENTS

- 1-Pound Loaf
- 1/3 Cup Milk
- 1/4 Cup Water
- 1 Large Egg
- Tablespoons Butter or Margarine, Cut Up
- 3/4 Teaspoon Salt
- 2-1/4 Cups Bread Flour
- Tablespoons Sugar
- 1-1/2 Teaspoons Fleischmann's Bread Machine Yeast

- 1-1/2-Pound Loaf
- 1/2 Cup Milk
- 1/3 Cup Water
- 1 Large Egg
- 1/4 Cup Butter or Margarine, Cut Up
- 1 Teaspoon Salt
- 3-1/3 Cups Bread Flour
- 1/4 Cup Sugar
- Teaspoons Fleischmann's Bread

DIRECTIONS

1. Put ingredients into bread machine pan.

NUTRITION

Calories: 130 calories;
Total Carbohydrate: 17 g

Total Fat: 5 g
Protein: 3 g

206. ALMOND AND CHOCOLATE CHIP BREAD

PREPARATION	COOKING	SERVES
10 MIN	3 HOURS 40 MIN	1 LOAF

INGREDIENTS

- 1 cup plus 2 tablespoons water
- tablespoons butter or margarine, softened
- ½ teaspoon vanilla
- cups Gold Medal™ Better for Bread™ flour
- ¾ cup semisweet chocolate chips
- tablespoons sugar

- 1 tablespoon dry milk
- ¾ teaspoon salt
- 1 ½ teaspoons bread machine or quick active dry yeast
- 1/3 cup sliced almonds

DIRECTIONS

1. Measure and put all ingredients except almonds in bread machine pan. Add almonds at the Nut signal or 5 – 10 minutes before kneading cycle ends.
2. Select White cycle. Use Light crust color.
3. Take out baked bread from pan.

NUTRITION

Calories: 130 calories;
Total Carbohydrate: 18 g
Total Fat: 7 g

Protein: 1 g
Protein: 3 g

207. SWEET PINEAPPLES BREAD

PREPARATION	COOKING	SERVES
120 MIN	40 MIN	5

INGREDIENTS

- oz. dried pineapples
- oz. raisins
- oz. wheat flour
- eggs

- teaspoon baking powder
- oz. brown sugar
- oz. sugar
- Vanilla

DIRECTIONS

1. Place the raisins into the warm water and leave for 20 minutes.
2. In a bowl, combine the sifted wheat flour, baking powder, brown sugar and vanilla.
3. Add the raisins and pineapples and mix well.
4. Whisk the eggs with the sugar until they have a smooth and creamy consistency.
5. Combine the eggs mixture with the flour and dried fruits mixture.
6. Pour the dough into the bread machine, close the lid and turn the bread machine on the basic/white bread program.
7. Bake the bread until the medium crust and after the bread is ready take it out and leave for 1 hour covered with the towel and only then you can slice the bread.

NUTRITION

Calories: 144 calories;
Total Carbohydrate: 18 g

Total Fat: 9 g
Protein: 6 g

208. SWEET COCONUT BREAD

PREPARATION	COOKING	SERVES
120 MIN	40 MIN	6

INGREDIENTS

- oz. shredded coconut
- oz. walnuts, ground
- oz. wheat flour
- oz. coconut butter
- eggs
- teaspoon baking powder
- oz. brown sugar
- Vanilla

DIRECTIONS

1. Whisk the eggs until they have a smooth and creamy consistency.
2. Combine the coconut butter with the brown sugar and vanilla and mix well, adding the eggs.
3. Combine the sifted wheat flour with the baking powder and eggs mixture and mix well until they have a smooth consistency.
4. Combine the dough with the shredded coconut and walnuts and then mix well.
5. Pour the dough into the bread machine, close the lid and turn the bread machine on the basic/white bread program.
6. Bake the bread until the medium crust and after the bread is ready take it out and leave for 1 hour covered with the towel and only then you can slice the bread.

NUTRITION

Calories: 164 calories;
Total Carbohydrate: 12 g

Total Fat: 8 g
Protein: 7 g

209. HONEY POUND CAKE

PREPARATION	COOKING	SERVES
5 MIN	2 HOURS 50 MIN	12-16

INGREDIENTS

- 1 cup butter, unsalted
- 1/4 cup honey
- Two tablespoons whole milk
- Four eggs, beaten
- 1 cup of sugar
- 2 cups flour

DIRECTIONS

1. Bring the butter to room temperature and cut into 1/2-inch cubes.
2. Add all ingredients to the bread machine in the order listed (butter, honey, milk, eggs, sugar, and flour).
3. Press Sweetbread setting follow by light crust color, then press Start. Take out the cake on the bread pan using a rubber spatula as soon as it's finished. Cool on a rack and serve with your favorite fruit.

NUTRITION

Calories: 117,
Sodium: 183 mg,
Dietary Fiber: 0.3 g,

Fat: 6.9 g,
Carbs: 12.3 g,
Protein: 1.9 g

210. CARROT CAKE BREAD

PREPARATION	COOKING	SERVES
5 MIN	80 MIN	12-16

INGREDIENTS

- Non-stick cooking spray
- 1/4 cup vegetable oil
- Two large eggs, room temperature
- 1/2 teaspoon pure vanilla extract
- 1/2 cup sugar
- 1/4 cup light brown sugar
- 1/4 cup of crushed pineapple with juice (from a can or fresh)
- 1 1/4 cups unbleached, all-purpose flour

- One teaspoon baking powder
- 1/4 teaspoon baking soda
- 1/4 teaspoon salt
- One teaspoon ground cloves
- 3/4 teaspoon ground cinnamon
- 1 cup freshly grated carrots
- 1/3 cup chopped pecans
- 1/3 cup golden raisins

DIRECTIONS

1. Coat the inside of the bread pan with non-stick cooking spray.
2. Add all of the ingredients, in the order listed, to the bread pan.
3. Select Express Bake, medium crust color, and press Start. While the batter is mixing, scrape the bread pan's sides with a rubber spatula to incorporate ingredients fully.
4. When baked, remove from bread pan and place on a wire rack to cool completely before slicing and serving.

NUTRITION

Calories: 151,
Sodium: 69 mg,
Dietary Fiber: 1.2 g,

Fat: 7.2 g,
Carbs: 20.1 g,
Protein: 2.4 g

211. LEMON CAKE

PREPARATION	COOKING	SERVES
5 MIN	2 HOURS 50 MIN	12

INGREDIENTS

- Three large eggs, beaten
- 1/3 cup 2% milk
- 1/2 cup butter, melted
- 2 cups all-purpose flour
- Three teaspoons baking powder
- 1 1/3 cup sugar
- One teaspoon vanilla extract
- Two lemons, zested
- For the glaze:
- 1 cup powdered sugar
- Two tablespoons lemon juice, freshly squeezed

DIRECTIONS

1. Prepare the glaze by whisking the powder sugar and lemon juice together in a small mixing bowl and set aside.
2. Add all remaining ingredients to the baking pan in the order listed.
3. Select the Sweetbread, medium color crust, and press Start.
4. When baked, transfer the baking pan to a cooling rack.
5. When the cake has cooled, gently shake the cake out into a serving plate. Glaze the cold cake and serve.

NUTRITION

Calories: 290
Sodium: 77 mg
Dietary Fiber: 0.6 g

Fat: 9.3 g
Carbs: 42.9 g
Protein: 4 g

212. INSANE COFFEE CAKE

PREPARATION	COOKING	SERVES
15 MIN	120 MIN	10-12

INGREDIENTS

- 7/8 cup of milk
- 1/4 cup of sugar
- One teaspoon salt
- One egg yolk
- One tablespoon butter
- 2 1/4 cups bread flour
- Two teaspoons of active dry yeast
- For the topping:
- Two tablespoons butter, melted
- Two tablespoons brown sugar
- One teaspoon cinnamon

DIRECTIONS

1. Set the topping ingredients set aside, then add the other ingredients to the bread pan in the order above.
2. Set the bread machine to the Dough process.
3. Butter a 9-by-9-inch glass baking dish and pour the dough into the container. Cover with a towel and rise for about 10 minutes.
4. Preheat an oven to 375°F.
5. Brush the dough with the melted butter.
6. Put brown sugar and cinnamon in a bowl, mix it well, and then put a sprinkle on top of the coffee cake.
7. Let the topped dough rise, uncovered, for another 30 minutes.
8. Place in oven and bake for 35 minutes or until a wooden toothpick inserted into the center comes out clean and dry.
9. When baked, let the coffee cake rest for 10 minutes. Carefully remove the coffee cake from the dish with a rubber spatula, slice and serve.

NUTRITION

Calories: 148
Sodium: 211 mg
Dietary Fiber: 0.9 g

Fat: 3.9 g
Carbs: 24.9 g
Protein: 3.5 g

213. CHOCOLATE MARBLE CAKE

PREPARATION	COOKING	SERVES
15 MIN	3 HOURS 45 MIN	12-16

INGREDIENTS

- 1 1/2 cups water
- 1 1/2 teaspoons vanilla extract
- 1 1/2 teaspoons salt
- 3 1/2 cups bread flour
- 1 1/2 teaspoons instant yeast
- 1 cup semi-sweet chocolate chips

DIRECTIONS

1. Set the chocolate chips aside and add the other ingredients to your bread maker's pan.
2. Program the machine for Sweetbread and then press Start.
3. Check the dough after 15 minutes of kneading; you should have a smooth ball, soft but not sticky.
4. Add the chocolate chips about 3 minutes before the end of the second kneading cycle.
5. Once baked, remove with a rubber spatula and cool on a rack before serving.

NUTRITION

Calories: 172
Sodium: 218 mg
Dietary Fiber: 1.6 g

Fat: 4.3 g
Carbs: 30.1 g
Protein: 3 g

214. PUMPKIN SPICE CAKE

PREPARATION	COOKING	SERVES
5 MIN	2 HOURS 50 MIN	12

INGREDIENTS

- 1 cup of sugar
- 1 cup canned pumpkin
- 1/3 cup vegetable oil
- One teaspoon vanilla extract
- Two eggs
- 1 1/2 cups all-purpose flour
- Two teaspoons baking powder
- 1/4 teaspoon salt
- One teaspoon ground cinnamon
- 1/4 teaspoon ground nutmeg
- 1/8 teaspoon ground cloves
- Shortening, for greasing pan

DIRECTIONS

1. Grease bread maker pan and kneading blade generously with shortening.
2. Add all ingredients to the pan in the order listed above.
3. Select the Rapid cycle and press Start.
4. Open the lid three minutes into the cycle,
5. Carefully scrape the pan's downsides with a rubber spatula; close the lid to continue the process.
6. Cool the baked cake for 10 minutes on a wire rack before slicing.

NUTRITION

Calories: 195
Sodium: 64 mg
Dietary Fiber: 1.3 g

Fat: 7.1 g
Carbs: 31.2 g
Protein: 2.8 g.

215. LEMON BLUEBERRY QUICK BREAD

PREPARATION	COOKING	SERVES
20 MIN	120 MIN	10-12

INGREDIENTS

- 2 cups all-purpose flour
- 1 1/2 teaspoons baking powder
- 1/2 teaspoon salt
- One tablespoon lemon zest
- 1 cup of sugar
- 1/2 cup unsalted butter, softened
- Two large eggs
- Two teaspoons pure vanilla extract
- 1/2 cup whole milk
- 1 1/2 cups blueberries
- For the crumb topping:
- 1/3 cup sugar
- Three tablespoons all-purpose flour
- Two tablespoons butter, melted
- Non-stick cooking spray

DIRECTIONS

1. Spray bread maker pan with non-stick cooking spray and lightly flour.
2. Combine crumb topping ingredients and set aside.
3. In a small bowl, put the whisk together with flour, baking powder and salt and set aside.
4. In a large bowl, put the sugar and lemon zest, then mix them. Add butter and beat until light and fluffy. Add eggs, vanilla and milk.
5. Add flour mixture and mix until combined. Stir in blueberries and spread batter evenly into bread maker pan.
6. Top with crumb topping; select Sweetbread, light color crust, and press Start.
7. When the cake is made, cool it on a wire rack for 15 minutes and serves warm.

NUTRITION

Calories: 462
Sodium: 332 mg
Dietary Fiber: 1 g

Fat: 32.1 g
Carbs: 41.8 g
Protein: 4 g

216. CINNAMON PECAN COFFEE CAKE

PREPARATION	COOKING	SERVES
15 MIN	120 MIN	10-12

INGREDIENTS

- 1 cup butter, unsalted
- 1 cup of sugar
- Two eggs
- 1 cup sour cream
- One teaspoon vanilla extract
- 2 cups all-purpose flour
- One teaspoon baking powder
- One teaspoon baking soda
- 1/2 teaspoon salt
- For the topping:
- 1/2 cup brown sugar
- 1/4 cup sugar
- 1/2 teaspoon cinnamon
- 1/2 cup pecans, chopped

DIRECTIONS

1. Add butter, sugar, eggs, sour cream and vanilla to the bread maker baking pan, followed by the dry ingredients.
2. Select the Cake cycle and press Start, then Prepare toppings and set aside.
3. When the kneading cycle is done, about 20 minutes, sprinkle 1/2 cup of topping on top of the dough and continue baking.
4. During the last hour of baking time, sprinkle the remaining 1/2 cup of topping on the cake. Bake until complete. Cool it on a wire rack for 10 minutes and serve warm.

NUTRITION

Calories: 488 Cal
Sodium: 333 mg

Fiber: 2.5 g
Fat: 32.8 g

FRUITY BREADS

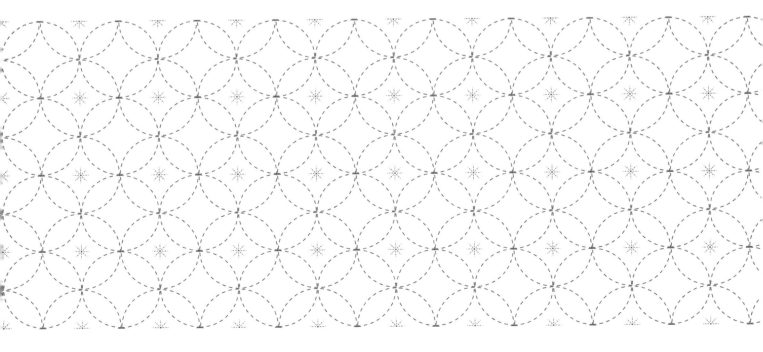

217. FRAGRANT ORANGE BREAD

PREPARATION	COOKING	SERVES
5 MIN	25 MIN	8

INGREDIENTS

- 1 cup milk,
- Three tablespoons freshly clasped orange juice
- Three tablespoons sugar
- One tablespoon melted butter cooled
- One teaspoon salt
- 3 cups white bread flour
- Zest of 1 orange
- 1¼ teaspoons bread machine or instant yeast

DIRECTIONS

1. Preparing the Ingredients. Place the ingredients in your Hamilton Beach bread machine.
2. Select the Bake cycle. Program the machine for Whitbread, choose the light or medium crust, and press Start. If the loaf is done, remove the bucket from the machine. Allow the loaf to cool for 5 minutes.
3. Moderately shake the pan to eliminate the loaf and turn it out onto a rack to cool.

NUTRITION

Calories 277
Cholesterol 9g
Carbohydrate 48.4g

Dietary Fiber 1.9g
Sugars 3.3g
Protein 9.4g

218. STRAWBERRY SHORTCAKE BREAD

PREPARATION	COOKING	SERVES
10 MIN	25 MIN	8

INGREDIENTS

- 1/2 cups milk, at 80°F to 90°F
- Three tablespoons melted butter, cooled
- Three tablespoons sugar
- 1½ teaspoons salt
- ¾ cup sliced fresh strawberries
- 1 cup quick oats
- 2¼ cups white bread flour
- 1½ teaspoons bread machine or instant yeast

DIRECTIONS

1. Preparing the Ingredients. Place the ingredients in your Hamilton Beach bread machine.
2. Select the Bake cycle. Program the machine for Whitbread, choose light or medium crust, and press Start.
3. If the loaf is done, remove the bucket from the machine.
4. Let the loaf cool for 5 minutes. Moderately shake the can to remove the loaf and turn it out onto a rack to cool.

NUTRITION

Calories 277
Cholesterol 9g
Carbohydrate 48.4g

Dietary Fiber 1.9g
Sugars 3.3g
Protein 9.4g

219. BLUEBERRY BREAD

PREPARATION	COOKING	SERVES
3 HOURS 15 MIN	40-45 MIN	1 LOAF

INGREDIENTS

- 1 1/8 to 1¼ cups Water
- 6 ounces Cream cheese, softened
- 2 tablespoons Butter or margarine
- ¼ cup Sugar
- 2 teaspoons Salt
- 4½ cups Bread flour
- 1½ teaspoons Grated lemon peel
- 2 teaspoons Cardamom
- 2 tablespoons Nonfat dry milk
- 2½ teaspoons Red star brand active dry yeast
- 2/3 cup dried blueberries

DIRECTIONS

1. Place all Ingredients except dried blueberries in bread pan, using the least amount of liquid listed in the recipe. Select light crust setting and the raisin / nut cycle. Press the start button.
2. Watch the dough as you knead. After 5 to 10 minutes, if it is dry and hard or if the machine seems to strain to knead it, add more liquid 1 tablespoon at a time until the dough forms a ball that is soft, tender, and slightly sticky to the touch.
3. When stimulated, add dried cranberries.
4. After the bake cycle is complete, remove the bread from the pan, place on the cake and allow to cool.

NUTRITION

Calories: 180 calories
Total Carbohydrate: 250 g

Fat: 3 g
Protein: 9 g

220. PINEAPPLE COCONUT BREAD

PREPARATION	COOKING	SERVES
10 MIN	25 MIN	8

INGREDIENTS

- Six tablespoons butter, at room temperature
- Two eggs, at room temperature
- ½ cup coconut milk, at room temperature
- ½ cup pineapple juice, at room temperature
- 1 cup of sugar
- 1½ teaspoons coconut extract
- 2 cups all-purpose flour
- ¾ cup shredded sweetened coconut
- One teaspoon baking powder
- ½ teaspoon salt

DIRECTIONS

1. Preparing the Ingredients. Place the butter, eggs, coconut milk, pineapple juice, sugar, and coconut extract in your Hamilton Beach bread machine.
2. Select the Bake cycle. Program the machine for Rapid bread and press Start. While the wet ingredients are mingling, stir together the flour, coconut, baking powder, and salt in a small bowl. After the first mixing is done and the machine motions, add the dry ingredients. When the loaf is done, eliminate the bucket from the machine. Let the loaf cool for 5 minutes. Slightly shake the pot to remove the loaf and turn it out onto a rack to cool.

NUTRITION

Calories 277
Cholesterol 9g
Carbohydrate 48.4g

Dietary Fiber 1.9g
Sugars 3.3g
Protein 9.4g

221. FRUIT SYRUP BREAD

PREPARATION	COOKING	SERVES
10 MIN	25 MIN	8

INGREDIENTS

- 3 2/3 cups whole wheat flour
- 1 1/2 tsp. instant yeast
- 1/4 cup unsalted butter, melted
- 1 cup lukewarm water
- 2 tbsp. sugar
- 1/4 cup rolled oats
- 1/2 tsp. salt
- 1/2 cup of syrup from preserved fruit

DIRECTIONS

1. Preparing the Ingredients. Combine the syrup and 1/2 cup water. Heat until lukewarm. Add more water to precisely 1 cup of water.
2. Place all the ingredients, except for the rolled oats and butter, in a liquid-dry-yeast layering.
3. Put the pan in the Hamilton Beach bread machine.
4. Load the rolled oats in the automatic dispenser.
5. Select the Bake cycle. Choose whole-wheat loaf.
6. Press start and wait until the loaf is cooked.
7. Brush the top with butter once cooked.
8. The machine will start the keep warm mode after the bread is complete.
9. Let it remain in that mode for about 10 minutes before unplugging.
10. Remove the pan and let it cool down for about 10 minutes.

NUTRITION

Calories 277
Cholesterol 9g
Carbohydrate 48.4g

Dietary Fiber 1.9g
Sugars 3.3g
Protein 9.4g

222. LEMON-LIME BLUEBERRY BREAD

PREPARATION	COOKING	SERVES
10 MIN	25 MIN	8

INGREDIENTS

- ¾ cup plain yogurt, at room temperature
- ½ cup of water
- Three tablespoons honey
- One tablespoon melted butter cooled
- 1½ teaspoons salt
- ½ teaspoon lemon extract
- One teaspoon lime zest
- 1 cup dried blueberries
- 3 cups white bread flour
- 2¼ teaspoons bread machine or instant yeast

DIRECTIONS

1. Preparing the Ingredients. Place the ingredients in your Hamilton Beach bread machine.
2. Select the Bake cycle. Program the machine for Whitbread, choose light or medium crust, then press Start.
3. Remove the bucket from the machine.
4. Let the loaf cool for 5 minutes.
5. Gently shake the pan to remove the loaf and turn it out onto a rack to cool.

NUTRITION

Calories 277
Cholesterol 9g
Carbohydrate 48.4g

Dietary Fiber 1.9g
Sugars 3.3g
Protein 9.4g

223. CRANBERRY YOGURT BREAD

PREPARATION	COOKING	SERVES
10 MIN	25 MIN	8

INGREDIENTS

- 3 cups + 2 tbsp. bread or all-purpose flour
- 1/2 cup lukewarm water
- 1 tbsp. olive or coconut oil
- 1 tbsp. orange or lemon essential oil
- 3 tbsp. sugar
- 3/4 cup yogurt
- 2 tsp. instant yeast
- 1 cup dried cried cranberries
- 1/2 cup raisins

DIRECTIONS

1. Preparing the Ingredients. Place all ingredients, except cranberries and raisins, in the bread pan in the liquid-dry-yeast layering.
2. Put the pan in the Hamilton Beach bread machine.
3. Load the fruits in the automatic dispenser.
4. Select the Bake cycle. Choose White bread.
5. Press start and wait until the loaf is cooked.
6. The machine will start the keep warm mode after the bread is complete.
7. Allow it to stay in that mode for at least 10 minutes before unplugging.
8. Remove the pan and let it cool down for about 10 minutes.

NUTRITION

Calories 277
Cholesterol 9g
Carbohydrate 48.4g

Dietary Fiber 1.9g
Sugars 3.3g
Protein 9.4g

224. PEACHES AND CREAM BREAD

PREPARATION	COOKING	SERVES
10 MIN	25 MIN	8

INGREDIENTS

- 3/4 cup canned peaches, drained and chopped
- 1/3 cup heavy whipping cream, at 80°F to 90°F
- One egg, at room temperature
- One tablespoon melted butter cooled
- Two 1/4 tablespoons sugar

- 1 1/8 teaspoons salt
- 1/3 teaspoon ground cinnamon
- 1/8 teaspoon ground nutmeg
- 1/3 cup whole-wheat flour
- 2 2/3 cups white bread flour
- 1 1/6 teaspoons bread machine or instant yeast

DIRECTIONS

1. Preparing the Ingredients. Place the ingredients in your Hamilton Beach bread machine.
2. Select the Bake cycle. Program the machine for Whitbread, select light or medium crust, and press Start.
3. When the loaf is done, eliminate the bucket from the machine.
4. Let the loaf cool for 5 minutes.
5. Shake the bucket to eliminate the loaf, and place it out onto a rack to cool.

NUTRITION

Calories 277
Cholesterol 9g
Carbohydrate 48.4g

Dietary Fiber 1.9g
Sugars 3.3g
Protein 9.4g

225. CINNAMON AND RAISIN PUMPERNICKEL BREAD

PREPARATION	COOKING	SERVES
10 MIN	25 MIN	8

INGREDIENTS

- 1 cup bread flour
- 1/3 cup rye flour
- 3/4 cup wheat flour
- 5/6 cup lukewarm water
- 2 tbsp. cocoa powder
- 6 tbsp. oil or melted shortening
- 1/2 tbsp. salt
- 1 tbsp. instant yeast
- 1/2 cup molasses
- 1/4 cup honey
- 1 1/2 tbsp. cinnamon
- 1 cup raisins

DIRECTIONS

1. Preparing the Ingredients. In a bowl, combine the water, molasses, salt, and oil. Stir until incorporated.
2. Place all ingredients, except raisins, in the bread pan in the liquid-dry-yeast layering.
3. Put the pan in the Hamilton Beach bread machine.
4. Load the raisins in the automatic dispenser
5. Select the Bake cycle. Choose Whole Wheat loaf.
6. Press start and wait until the loaf is cooked.
7. The machine will start the keep warm mode after the bread is complete.
8. Make it stay in that mode for about 10 minutes before unplugging.
9. Remove the pan and let it cool down for about 10 minutes.

NUTRITION

Calories 277
Cholesterol 9g
Carbohydrate 48.4g

Dietary Fiber 1.9g
Sugars 3.3g
Protein 9.4g

226. BANANA BREAD

PREPARATION	COOKING	SERVES	DIFFICULTY
100 MIN	40-45 MIN	1 LOAF	BEGINNERS

INGREDIENTS

- 1 teaspoon Baking powder
- 1/2 teaspoon Baking soda
- bananas, peeled and halved lengthwise
- cups all-purpose flour
- eggs
- tablespoon Vegetable oil
- 3/4 cup white sugar

DIRECTIONS

1. Put all the Ingredients in the bread pan. Select dough setting. Start and mix for about 3-5 minutes.
2. After 3-5 minutes, press stop. Do not continue to mix. Smooth out the top of the dough
3. Using the spatula and then select bake, start and bake for about 50 minutes. After 50 minutes, insert a toothpick into the top center to test doneness.
4. Remove bread and cool in wire rack.

NUTRITION

Calories: 310 calories
Total Carbohydrate: 40 g
Fat: 13 g
Protein: 3 g

227. ORANGE AND WALNUT BREAD

PREPARATION	COOKING	SERVES	DIFFICULTY
2 HOURS 50 MIN	45 MIN	10-15	BEGINNERS

INGREDIENTS

- 1 egg white
- 1 tablespoon water
- ½ cup warm whey
- 1 tablespoons yeast
- tablespoons sugar
- oranges, crushed
- cups flour

- 1 teaspoon salt
- 1 and ½ tablespoon salt
- teaspoons orange peel
- 1/3 teaspoon vanilla
- tablespoons walnut and almonds, crushed
- Crushed pepper, salt, cheese for garnish

DIRECTIONS

1. Add all of the ingredients to your Bread Machine (except egg white, 1 tablespoon water and crushed pepper/ cheese).
2. Set the program to "Dough" cycle and let the cycle run.
3. Remove the dough (using lightly floured hands) and carefully place it on a floured surface.
4. Cover with a light film/cling paper and let the dough rise for 10 minutes.
5. Divide the dough into thirds after it has risen
6. Place on a lightly flour surface, roll each portion into 14x10 inch sized rectangles
7. Use a sharp knife to cut carefully cut the dough into strips of ½ inch width
8. Pick 2-3 strips and twist them multiple times, making sure to press the ends together
9. Preheat your oven to 400 degrees F
10. Take a bowl and stir egg white, water and brush onto the breadsticks
11. Sprinkle salt, pepper/ cheese
12. Bake for 10-12 minutes until golden brown
13. Remove from baking sheet and transfer to cooling rack Serve and enjoy!

NUTRITION

Calories: 437 calories;
Total Carbohydrate: 82 g
Total Fat: 7 g

Protein: 12 g
Sugar: 34 g
Fiber: 1 g

228. LEMON AND POPPY BUNS

PREPARATION	COOKING	SERVES	DIFFICULTY
2 HOURS 50 MIN	45 MIN	10-20 BUNS	BEGINNERS

INGREDIENTS

- Melted Butter for grease
- 1 and 1/3 cups hot water
- tablespoons powdered milk
- tablespoons Crisco shortening
- 1 and ½ teaspoon salt
- 1 tablespoon lemon juice

- and ¼ cups bread flour
- ½ teaspoon nutmeg
- teaspoons grated lemon rind
- tablespoons poppy seeds
- 1 and ¼ teaspoons yeast
- teaspoons wheat gluten

DIRECTIONS

1. Add all of the ingredients to your Bread Machine (except melted butter).
2. Set the program to "Dough" cycle and let the cycle run.
3. Remove the dough (using lightly floured hands) and carefully place it on a floured surface.
4. Cover with a light film/cling paper and let the dough rise for 10 minutes.
5. Take a large cookie sheet and grease with butter.
6. Cut the risen dough into 15-20 pieces and shape them into balls.
7. Place the balls onto the sheet (2 inches apart) and cover.
8. Place in a warm place and let them rise for 30-40 minutes until the dough doubles.
9. Preheat your oven to 375 degrees F, transfer the cookie sheet to your oven and bake for 12-15 minutes. Brush the top with a bit of butter, enjoy!

NUTRITION

Calories: 231 calories;
Total Carbohydrate: 31 g
Total Fat: 11 g

Protein: 4 g
Sugar: 12 g
Fiber: 1 g

229. APPLE WITH PUMPKIN BREAD

PREPARATION	COOKING	SERVES	DIFFICULTY
2 HOURS 50 MIN	45 MIN	2 LOAVES	BEGINNERS

INGREDIENTS

- 1/3 cup dried apples, chopped
- 1 1/2 teaspoon bread machine yeast
- cups bread flour
- 1/3 cup ground pecans
- 1/4 teaspoon ground nutmeg
- 1/4 teaspoon ground ginger
- 1/4 teaspoon allspice
- 1/2 teaspoon ground cinnamon
- 1 1/4 teaspoon salt
- tablespoon unsalted butter, cubed
- 1/3 cup dry skim milk powder
- 1/4 cup honey
- large eggs, at room temperature
- 2/3 cup pumpkin puree
- 2/3 cup water, with a temperature of 80 to 90 degrees F (26 to 32 degrees C)

DIRECTIONS

1. Put all ingredients, except the dried apples, in the bread pan in this order: water, pumpkin puree, eggs, honey, skim milk, butter, salt, allspice, cinnamon, pecans, nutmeg, ginger, flour, and yeast.
2. Secure the pan in the machine and lock the lid.
3. Place the dried apples in the fruit and nut dispenser.
4. Turn on the machine. Choose the sweet setting and your desired color of the crust.
5. Carefully unmold the baked bread once done and allow to cool for 20 minutes before slicing.

NUTRITION

Calories: 228 calories;
Total Carbohydrate: 30 g

Total Fat: 4 g
Protein: 18 g

230. WARM SPICED PUMPKIN BREAD

PREPARATION	COOKING	SERVES	DIFFICULTY
2 HOURS	15 MIN	12-16	BEGINNERS

INGREDIENTS

- Butter for greasing the bucket
- 1½ cups pumpkin purée
- eggs, at room temperature
- ⅓ cup melted butter, cooled
- 1 cup sugar
- cups all-purpose flour
- 1½ teaspoons baking powder
- ¾ teaspoon ground cinnamon
- ½ teaspoon baking soda
- ¼ teaspoon ground nutmeg
- ¼ teaspoon ground ginger
- ¼ teaspoon salt
- Pinch ground cloves

DIRECTIONS

1. Lightly grease the bread bucket with butter.
2. Add the pumpkin, eggs, butter, and sugar.
3. Program the machine for Quick/Rapid bread and press Start.
4. Let the wet ingredients be mixed by the paddles until the first fast mixing cycle is finished, about 10 minutes into the cycle.
5. When the loaf is done, remove the bucket from the machine.
6. Let the loaf cool for 5 minutes.
7. Gently shake the bucket to remove the loaf, and turn it out onto a rack to cool.

NUTRITION

Calories: 251 calories;
Total Carbohydrate: 43 g
Total Fat: 7 g

Protein: 5 g
Sodium: 159 mg
Fiber: 2 g

231. PURE PEACH BREAD

PREPARATION	COOKING	SERVES	DIFFICULTY
2 HOURS	15 MIN	12	BEGINNERS

INGREDIENTS

- ¾ cup peaches, chopped
- ⅓ cup heavy whipping cream
- 1 egg
- 1 tablespoon butter, melted at room temperature
- ⅓ teaspoon ground cinnamon
- ⅛ teaspoon ground nutmeg
- ¼ tablespoons sugar
- 1 ⅛ teaspoons salt
- ⅓ cup whole-wheat flour
- ⅔ cups white bread flour
- 1 ⅛ teaspoons instant or bread machine yeast

DIRECTIONS

1. Take 1 ½ pound size loaf pan and first add the liquid ingredients and then add the dry ingredients.
2. Place the loaf pan in the machine and close its top lid.
3. For selecting a bread cycle, press "Basic Bread/White Bread/Regular Bread" and for selecting a crust type, press "Light" or "Medium".
4. Start the machine and it will start preparing the bread.
5. After the bread loaf is completed, open the lid and take out the loaf pan.
6. Allow the pan to cool down for 10-15 minutes on a wire rack. Gently shake the pan and remove the bread loaf.
7. Make slices and serve.

NUTRITION

Calories: 51 calories;
Total Carbohydrate: 12 g
Cholesterol: 0 g

Total Fat: 0.3 g
Protein: 1.20 g
Fiber: 2 g

232. DATE DELIGHT BREAD

PREPARATION	COOKING	SERVES	DIFFICULTY
2 HOURS	15 MIN	12	BEGINNERS

INGREDIENTS

- ¾ cup water, lukewarm
- ½ cup milk, lukewarm
- tablespoons butter, melted at room temperature
- ¼ cup honey
- tablespoons molasses
- 1 tablespoon sugar
- ¼ cups whole-wheat flour
- 1 ¼ cups white bread flour
- tablespoons skim milk powder
- 1 teaspoon salt
- 1 tablespoon unsweetened cocoa powder
- 1 ½ teaspoons instant or bread machine yeast
- ¾ cup chopped dates

DIRECTIONS

1. Take 1 ½ pound size loaf pan and first add the liquid ingredients and then add the dry ingredients. (Do not add the dates as of now.)
2. Place the loaf pan in the machine and close its top lid.
3. Plug the bread machine into power socket. For selecting a bread cycle, press "Basic Bread/ White Bread/Regular Bread" or "Fruit/Nut Bread" and for selecting a crust type, press "Light" or "Medium".
4. Start the machine and it will start preparing the bread. When machine beeps or signals, add the dates.
5. After the bread loaf is completed, open the lid and take out the loaf pan.
6. Allow the pan to cool down for 10-15 minutes on a wire rack. Gently shake the pan and remove the bread loaf.
7. Make slices and serve.

NUTRITION

Calories: 220 calories;
Total Carbohydrate: 52 g
Cholesterol: 0 g

Total Fat: 5 g
Protein: 4 g

233. BLUEBERRY HONEY BREAD

PREPARATION	COOKING	SERVES	DIFFICULTY
2 HOURS	15 MIN	12	BEGINNERS

INGREDIENTS

- ¾ cup milk, lukewarm
- 1 egg, at room temperature
- ¼ tablespoons butter, melted at room temperature
- 1 ½ tablespoons honey
- ½ cup rolled oats
- ⅓ cups white bread flour
- 1 ⅛ teaspoons salt
- 1 ½ teaspoons instant or bread machine yeast
- ½ cup dried blueberries

DIRECTIONS

1. Take 1 ½ pound size loaf pan and first add the liquid ingredients and then add the dry ingredients. (Do not add the blueberries as of now.)
2. Place the loaf pan in the machine and close its top lid.
3. Plug the bread machine into power socket. For selecting a bread cycle, press "Basic Bread/White Bread/Regular Bread" or "Fruit/Nut Bread" and for selecting a crust type, press "Light" or "Medium".
4. Start the machine and it will start preparing the bread. When machine beeps or signals, add the blueberries.
5. After the bread loaf is completed, open the lid and take out the loaf pan.
6. Allow the pan to cool down for 10-15 minutes on a wire rack. Gently shake the pan and remove the bread loaf.
7. Make slices and serve.

NUTRITION

Calories: 180 calories;
Total Carbohydrate: 250 g

Total Fat: 3 g
Protein: 9 g

PIZZA DOUGH

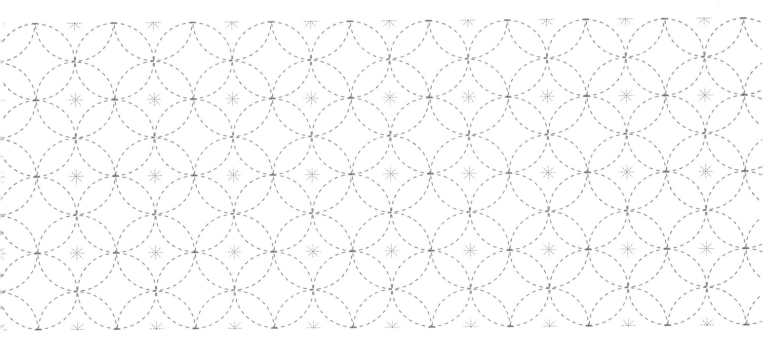

234. PIZZA DOUGH

PREPARATION	COOKING	SERVES
10 MIN	90 MIN	2

INGREDIENTS

- 1 cup of warm water
- ¾ teaspoon salt
- 2 tablespoons olive oil
- 2 ½ cups flour
- 2 teaspoons sugar
- 2 teaspoons yeast

DIRECTIONS

1. Put ingredients in the bread maker.
2. Enable the Dough program and start the cycle.
3. Put the finished dough in a greased form or pan and distribute it. Allow standing for 10 minutes.
4. Preheat the oven to 400°F. On top of the dough, place the pizza sauce and the filling. Top with grated cheese.
5. For 15 to 20 minutes, bake till the edge is browned.

NUTRITION

Calories 716;
Total Fat 15.7g;
Saturated Fat 2.3g;
Cholesterol 0mg;
Sodium 881g;

Total Carbohydrate 124.8g;
Dietary Fiber 5.1g;
Total Sugars 4.4 g;
Protein 17.7g

235. PIZZA BASIS

PREPARATION	COOKING	SERVES
10 MIN	80 MIN	2

INGREDIENTS

- 1 ¼ cups warm water
- 2 cups flour
- 1 cup Semolina flour
- ½ teaspoon sugar
- 1 teaspoon salt
- 1 teaspoon olive oil
- 2 teaspoons yeast

DIRECTIONS

1. Place all the ingredients in the bread maker's bucket in the order recommended by the manufacturer. Select the Dough program.
2. After the dough has risen, use it as the base for the pizza.

NUTRITION

Calories 718;
Total Fat 4.4g;
Saturated Fat 0.6g;
Cholesterol 0mg;
Sodium 1173g;

Total Carbohydrate 145.6g;
Dietary Fiber 5.9g;
Total Sugars 1.5 g;
Protein 20.9g

236. CINNAMON RAISIN BUNS

PREPARATION	COOKING	SERVES
10 MIN	45 MIN	12

INGREDIENTS

- For dough
- ½ cup milk
- ½ cup of water
- 2 tablespoons butter
- ¾ teaspoon salt
- 3 cups flour
- 2 ¼ teaspoon yeast
- 3 tablespoons sugar
- 1 egg
- For filling

- 3 tablespoons butter, melted
- ¾ teaspoon ground cinnamon
- 1/3 cup sugar
- 1/3 cup raisins
- 1/3 cup chopped walnuts
- For glaze
- 1 cup powdered sugar
- 1 ½ tablespoon melted butter
- ¼ teaspoon vanilla
- 1 ½ tablespoons milk

NUTRITION

Calories 308;
Total Fat 9.2g;
Saturated Fat 4.3g;
Cholesterol 31mg;
Sodium 202g;
Total Carbohydrate 53.2g;
Dietary Fiber 1.5g;
Total Sugars 27.9 g;
Protein 5.2g

DIRECTIONS

1. In a saucepan, heat ½ cup of milk, water, and 2 tablespoons of butter until they become hot.
2. Put the milk mixture, salt, flour, yeast, sugar, and eggs in the bread maker's bucket in the order recommended by the manufacturer. Select the Dough program. Click Start.
3. When through with the cycle, take out the dough from the bread maker. On a flour-covered surface, roll the dough into a large rectangle. Lubricate with softened butter.
4. Mix the cinnamon and sugar. Sprinkle the rectangle with the mixture. Generously sprinkle with raisins and/or chopped nuts.
5. Roll the dough into a roll, starting from the long side. Cut into 12 pieces. Put the buns slit-side down on a greased baking tray (25x35cm).
6. Cover and put in the heat until the dough almost doubles, about 30 minutes.
7. Preheat the oven to 375 degree F. Mix the powdered sugar, 1 1/2 tablespoon melted butter, vanilla, and 1 ½ tablespoon milk to get a thick frosting; set it aside.
8. Bake the buns in a preheated oven for 20 - 25 minutes, until browned. Remove and allow to cool down for 10 minutes. Frost the cooled buns with icing.

237. ITALIAN PIE CALZONE

PREPARATION	COOKING	SERVES
5 MIN	65 MIN	12

INGREDIENTS

- 1 ¼ cups water
- 1 teaspoon salt
- 3 cups flour
- 1 teaspoon milk powder
- 1 ½ tablespoons sugar
- 2 teaspoons yeast
- ¾ cup tomato sauce for pizza
- 1 cup pepperoni sausage, finely chopped
- 1 ¼ cups grated mozzarella
- 2 tablespoons butter, melted

NUTRITION

Calories 247;
Total Fat 9.2g;
Saturated Fat 3.9g;
Cholesterol 22mg;
Sodium 590g;
Total Carbohydrate 32g;
Dietary Fiber 1.5g;
Total Sugars 2.8 g;
Protein 8.6g

DIRECTIONS

1. Put water, salt, bread baking flour, soluble milk, sugar, and yeast in the bread maker's bucket in the order recommended by the manufacturer. Select the Dough setting.

2. After the end of the cycle, roll the dough on a lightly floured surface; form a rectangle measuring 45 x 25 cm. Transfer to a lightly oiled baking tray.

3. In a small bowl, combine the chopped pepperoni and mozzarella. Spoon the pizza sauce in a strip along the center of the dough. Add the filling of sausage and cheese.

4. Make diagonal incisions at a distance of 1 ½ cm from each other at the sides, receding 1 ½ cm from the filling.

5. Cross the strips on top of the filling, moistening it with the water. Lubricate with melted butter.

6. For 35 to 45 minutes bake at 360 degree F.

238. FRENCH BAGUETTES

PREPARATION	COOKING	SERVES
20 MIN	150 MIN	6

INGREDIENTS

- 1½ cups water
- 1½ teaspoons sugar
- 1½ teaspoons salt
- 3½ cups flour
- 1½ teaspoons yeast
- a mixture of different seeds (pumpkin, sunflower, black and white sesame)

NUTRITION

Calories 272;
Total Fat 0.8g;
Saturated Fat 0.1g;
Cholesterol 0mg;
Sodium 585g;
Total Carbohydrate 57g;
Dietary Fiber 2.2g;
Total Sugars 1.2g;
Protein 7.9g

DIRECTIONS

1. To prepare the dough for French baguettes in the bread maker, place all the ingredients in the bread maker's container in order: water, salt, and sugar, flour, yeast. Select the Yeast Dough program.
2. After 1½ hour, the dough for baguettes is ready.
3. Heat the oven to 440°F. Divide the dough into 2 parts. Lubricate the pan with oil. From the dough, form two French baguettes. Put on a baking pan and let it come for 10 minutes.
4. Then with a sharp knife, make shallow incisions on the surface of the baguettes. Sprinkle with water and sprinkle with a mixture of seeds. Leave it for another 10 minutes.
5. After the oven is warmed, put the pan with French baguettes in the oven for 5-7 minutes, then lower the heat to 360°F and bake for another 20-30 minutes until ready.
6. Transfer baguettes to a grate and cool.
7. Your crispy, delicious, fragrant French baguettes are ready... Bon Appetit!

239. CHEDDAR BISCUITS

PREPARATION	COOKING	SERVES
10 MIN	25 MIN	12

INGREDIENTS

- eggs
- ¼ cup unsalted butter, melted
- 1 ¼ cups, coconut milk
- ¼ tsp. salt
- ¼ tsp. baking soda
- ¼ tsp. garlic powder
- ½ cup finely shredded sharp cheddar cheese
- 1 Tbsp. fresh herb
- 2/3 cup coconut flour

DIRECTIONS

1. Preheat the oven to 350F. Grease a baking sheet.
2. Mix together the butter, eggs, milk, salt, baking soda, garlic powder, cheese, and herbs until well blended.
3. Add the coconut flour to the batter and mix until well blended. Let the batter sit then mix again.
4. Spoon about 2 tbsp. batter for each biscuit onto the greased baking sheet.
5. Bake for 25 minutes.
6. Serve warm.

NUTRITION

Calories: 125
Fat: 7g

Carb: 10g
Protein: 5g

240. SAVORY WAFFLES

PREPARATION	COOKING	SERVES
10 MIN	20 MIN	4XX

INGREDIENTS

- eggs
- 1 tsp. olive oil
- ½ cup sliced scallions
- ¾ cup grated pepper Jack cheese
- ¼ tsp. baking soda
- Pinch salt
- Tbsp. coconut flour

DIRECTIONS

1. Preheat the waffle iron to medium heat.
2. Mix all the ingredients using a bowl. Let the batter sit and mix once more.
3. Scoop ½ cup to 1-cup batter (depending on the size of the waffle iron) and pour onto the iron. Cook according to the manufacturer's directions.
4. Serve warm.

NUTRITION

Calories: 183
Fat: 13g

Carb: 4g
Protein: 12g

241. CHOCOLATE CHIP SCONES

PREPARATION	COOKING	SERVES
10 MIN	10 MIN	8

INGREDIENTS

- cups almond flour
- 1 tsp. baking soda
- ¼ tsp. sea salt
- 1 egg

- Tbsp. low-carb sweetener
- Tbsp. milk, cream or yogurt
- ½ cup sugar-free chocolate chips

DIRECTIONS

1. Preheat the oven to 350F.
2. Using a bowl, add almond flour, baking soda, and salt and blend.
3. Then add the egg, sweetener, milk, and chocolate chips. Blend well.
4. Tap the dough into a ball and place it on parchment paper.
5. Roll the dough with a rolling pin into a large circle. Slice it into 8 triangular pieces.
6. Place the scones and parchment paper on a baking sheet and separate the scones about 1 inch or so apart.
7. For 7 to 10 minutes, bake until lightly browned.
8. Cool and serve.

NUTRITION

Calories: 213
Fat: 18g

Carb: 10g
Protein: 8g

242. SNICKERDOODLES

PREPARATION	COOKING	SERVES
10 MIN	10 MIN	20

INGREDIENTS

- cups almond flour
- Tbsp. coconut flour
- ¼ tsp. baking soda
- ¼ tsp. salt
- Tbsp. unsalted butter, melted

- 1/3 cup low-carb sweetener
- ¼ cup coconut milk
- 1 Tbsp. vanilla extract
- Tbsp. ground cinnamon
- Tbsp. low-carb granulated sweetener

DIRECTIONS

1. Preheat the oven to 350F.
2. Whisk the almond flour, coconut flour, salt and baking soda together using a bowl.
3. In another bowl, cream the butter, sweetener, milk and vanilla.
4. Put the flour mixture to the butter mixture and blend well.
5. Line baking sheets with parchment paper.
6. Blend the ground cinnamon and low-carb granulated sweetener together in a bowl. With your hands, roll a tbsp. of dough into a ball.
7. Reel the dough ball in the cinnamon mixture to fully coat.
8. Put the dough balls on the cookie sheet, spread about an inch apart, and flatten with the underside of a jar.
9. Bake for 8 to 10 minutes.
10. Cool and serve.

NUTRITION

Calories: 86
Fat: 7g

Carb: 3g
Protein: 3g

243. NO CORN CORNBREAD

PREPARATION	COOKING	SERVES
10 MIN	20 MIN	8

INGREDIENTS

- ½ cup almond flour
- ¼ cup coconut flour
- ¼ tsp. salt
- ¼ tsp. baking soda
- eggs
- ¼ cup unsalted butter
- Tbsp. low-carb sweetener
- ½ cup coconut milk

DIRECTIONS

1. Preheat the oven to 325F. Line a baking pan.
2. Combine dry ingredients in a bowl.
3. Put all the dry ingredients to the wet ones and blend well.
4. Dispense the batter into the baking pan and bake for 20 minutes.
5. Cool, slice, and serve.

NUTRITION

Calories: 65
Fat: 6g

Carb: 2g
Protein: 2g

244. GARLIC CHEESE BREAD LOAF

PREPARATION	COOKING	SERVES
10 MIN	45 MIN	10

INGREDIENTS

- 1 Tbsp. parsley, chopped
- ½ cup butter, unsalted and softened
- Tbsp. garlic powder
- large eggs
- ½ tsp. oregano seasoning
- 1 tsp. baking powder
- cups almond flour
- ½ tsp. xanthan gum
- 1 cup cheddar cheese, shredded
- ½ tsp. salt

DIRECTIONS

1. Preheat the oven to 355F.
2. Line a baking pan with parchment paper.
3. In a food blender, pulse the eggs until smooth. Then combine the butter and pulse for 1 minute more.
4. Blend the almond flour and baking powder for 90 seconds or until thickens.
5. Finally, combine the garlic, oregano, parsley, and cheese until mixed.
6. Pour into the prepared and bake in the oven for 45 minutes.
7. Cool, slice, and serve.

NUTRITION

Calories: 299
Fat: 27g

Carb: 4g
Protein: 11g

245. IRANIAN FLAT BREAD (SANGAK)

PREPARATION	COOKING	SERVES
3 HOURS	15 MIN	6

INGREDIENTS

- cups almond flour
- ½ cups warm water
- 1 Tbsp. instant yeast
- tsp. sesame seeds
- Salt to taste

DIRECTIONS

1. Add 1 tbsp. yeast to ½ cup warm water using a bowl and allow to stand for 5 minutes.
2. Add salt add 1 cup of water. Let stand for 10 minutes longer.
3. Put one cup of flour at a time, and then add the remaining water.
4. Knead the dough and then shape into a ball and let stand for 3 hours covered.
5. Preheat the oven to 480F.
6. By means of a rolling pin, roll out the dough, and divide into 6 balls.
7. Roll each ball into ½ inch thick rounds.
8. Place a parchment paper on the baking sheet and place the rolled rounds on it.
9. With a finger, make a small hole in the middle and add 2 tsp sesame seeds in each hole.
10. Bake for 3 to 4 minutes, then flip over and bake for 2 minutes more.
11. Serve.

NUTRITION

Calories: 26
Fat: 1g

Carb: 3.5g
Protein: 0.7g

246. CHOCOLATE ZUCCHINI BREAD

PREPARATION	COOKING	SERVES
10 MIN	20 MIN	10

INGREDIENTS

- cups grated zucchini, excess moisture removed
- eggs
- Tbsp. olive oil
- 1/3 cup low-carb sweetener
- 1 tsp. vanilla extract
- 1/3 cup coconut flour
- ¼ cup unsweetened cocoa powder
- ½ tsp. baking soda
- ½ tsp. salt
- 1/3 cup sugar-free chocolate chips

DIRECTIONS

1. Preheat the oven to 350F.
2. Grease the baking pan and line the entire pan with parchment paper.
3. In a food processor, blend the eggs, zucchini, oil, sweetener, and vanilla.
4. Add the flour, cocoa, baking soda, and salt to the zucchini mixture and stir until mixed. For a few seconds, let the batter sit.
5. Mix in the chocolate chips, then dispense the batter into the prepared pan.
6. Bake for 45 to 50 minutes.
7. Cool, slice, and serve.

NUTRITION

Calories: 149
Fat: 8g
Carb: 7g
Protein: 3g

247. CAULIFLOWER BREADSTICKS

PREPARATION	COOKING	SERVES
10 MIN	35 MIN	8

INGREDIENTS

- cups riced cauliflower
- 1 cup mozzarella, shredded
- 1 tsp. Italian seasoning
- eggs
- ½ tsp. ground pepper
- 1 tsp. salt
- ½ tsp. granulated garlic
- ¼ cup Parmesan cheese as a topping

DIRECTIONS

1. Preheat the oven to 350F. Grease a baking sheet.
2. Beat the eggs until mixed well.
3. Combine riced cauliflower, mozzarella cheese, Italian seasoning, pepper, garlic, and salt and blend on low speed in a food processor. Combine with eggs.
4. Pour the dough into the prepared cookie sheet and pat the dough down to ¼ thick across the pan.
5. Bake for 30 minutes and dust the breadsticks with the parmesan cheese.
6. Put the breadsticks on the broil setting for 2 to 3 minutes, so the cheese melts.
7. Slice and serve.

NUTRITION

Calories: 165
Fat: 10g

Carb: 5g
Protein: 13g

248. CHEDDAR CRACKERS

PREPARATION	COOKING	SERVES
10 MIN	55 MIN	8

INGREDIENTS

- Tbsp. unsalted butter, softened slightly
- 1 egg white
- ¼ tsp. salt
- 1 cup plus 2 Tbsp. almond flour
- 1 tsp. minced fresh thyme
- 1 cup shredded sharp white cheddar cheese

DIRECTIONS

1. Preheat the oven to 300F.
2. Using a bowl, beat together the butter, egg white, and salt.
3. Stir in the almond flour, and thyme and then the cheddar until mixed.
4. Move the dough out between two pieces of parchment paper to a rectangle.
5. Peel off the top parchment paper and place the dough with the bottom parchment paper on a sheet pan.
6. Cut the dough into crackers with a pizza cutter.
7. Bake until golden, about 45 to 55 minutes, rotating the tray once halfway through.
8. Cool and serve.

NUTRITION

Calories: 200
Fat: 18g

Carb: 4g
Protein: 7g

249. SESAME ALMOND CRACKERS

PREPARATION	COOKING	SERVES
10 MIN	24 MIN	8

INGREDIENTS

- Tbsp. unsalted butter, softened slightly
- egg whites
- ½ tsp. salt
- ¼ tsp. black pepper
- ¼ cups almond flour
- Tbsp. sesame seeds

DIRECTIONS

1. Preheat the oven to 350F.
2. Using a bowl, beat the egg whites, butter, salt, and black pepper.
3. Stir in the almond flour and sesame seeds.
4. Move the dough out between two pieces of parchment paper to a rectangle.
5. Peel off the top parchment paper and place the dough on a sheet pan.
6. Cut the dough into crackers with a pizza cutter.
7. Bake for 18 to 24 minutes, or until golden, rotating the tray halfway through.
8. Serve.

NUTRITION

Calories: 299
Fat: 28g

Carb: 4g
Protein: 8g

250. NO-YEAST SOURDOUGH STARTER

PREPARATION	COOKING	SERVES
10 MIN	0 MIN	64

INGREDIENTS

- cups all-purpose flour
- cups chlorine-free bottled water, at room temperature

DIRECTIONS

1. Stir together the flour and water in a large glass bowl with a wooden spoon.
2. With a plastic wrap, put a cover the bowl and place it in a warm area for 3 to 4 days, stirring at least twice a day, or until bubbly.
3. Store the starter in the refrigerator in a covered glass jar, and stir it before using.
4. Replenish your starter by adding back the same amount you removed, in equal parts flour and water.

NUTRITION

Calories: 14
Fat: 0g
Carbohydrates: 3g

Fiber: 0g
Protein: 0g

TROUBLESHOOTING

Every kitchen appliance has problems, especially if you've been using it for a while. Because bread-making is such an exact science, there are quite a few things that can go wrong that actually have nothing to do with your machine's performance. Here's the most common problems bread-machine users encounter and what to do about them:

Problem: Bread didn't rise

Solution: Bread doesn't rise for a number of reasons. The first thing is that you measured incorrectly or maybe even accidentally forgot an ingredient. The yeast, which creates rise, may be the problem, especially if you've had it in your cupboard for a long time. Yeast can get old or go bad if it isn't stored correctly. To ensure it lasts a long time, keep it in the freezer. It doesn't need to be warmed or anything before use, you can use it right from the cold. Yeast can also die if you used too much water, too much salt, or too much sugar.

What if the bread did rise, but the loaf is shorter than you would like? You might not have used enough sugar and the yeast didn't have enough to eat. It's also possible that the yeast was old or bad. If the loaf is whole-grain or you used all-purpose flour, a shorter and heavier result is normal. In the future, check the consistency of the dough five minutes into the kneading process (you can interrupt the machine) and see if it's too dry. If it is, you can add a one tablespoon of liquid at a time. Using a high-protein bread flour can also help with heaviness. The last reason for a loaf with a low rise is that the bread pan is too large, so the dough didn't fill it while it baked.

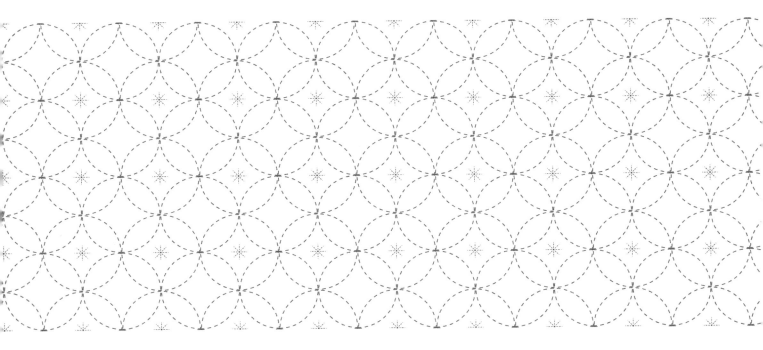

Problem: Top of bread has a "mushroom" top

<u>Solution</u>: If your bread ends up with an odd-shaped top that resembles a mushroom, the most common reason is that your ingredients were out of proportion. This could mean too much flour, too much liquid, too much salt, too much sugar, or too much yeast. The next time you make the recipe, read the instructions very carefully and be especially cautious when measuring. If you're using a recipe you converted yourself, figuring out which ingredient is out of proportion will be pretty difficult. It's better to find a recipe that people have found success with.

Problem: Top of the loaf sunk or collapsed

<u>Solution</u>: The primary reason for bread with a sunken top is too much water. This made the dough too soft, so that during baking, it was unable to hold its shape and sunk. Another problem could be that the water was too warm when you added it to the yeast, so the dough rose too quickly and sank before or soon after the baking process began. Use cool, even cold, liquids. Humidity and hot water speed up the yeast, as well, so try baking during the coolest part of the day.

If you've ruled out liquid as the culprit, it could be that you didn't use enough salt. Add more next time you make the recipe. Did you open the bread machine during the baking cycle at any point? This can cause sinkage. A bread pan that's too small can also result in a sunken loaf.

Problem: Crust is too thick and/or too dark

<u>Solution</u>: These issues have easy solutions. If the crust is too thick, it's just hanging out in the bread machine for too long, so as soon as the baking cycle is done, take it out. If the crust is darker than you like, just try a lighter crust-color setting. Not every machine has this feature; if yours doesn't, just take it out a very minutes before the baking cycle is over. The bread will continue to bake because of residual heat, but the crust won't get too dark.

Problem: Coarse texture

Solution: The reason your bread is too coarse could be you used too much liquid. If your bread has any fruit or veggies in it, their liquid content could be affecting the bread. Decrease the amount of liquid you use next time you make the recipe, and be sure to pat the fruits/veggies dry after rinsing them. Coarseness can also be caused by too much yeast or yeast that worked too quickly because of hot weather or too-warm ingredients. Use less yeast next time or if you believe heat was the driving factor, be sure to use cooler ingredients and bake during the cooler part of the day. Lastly, be sure to use salt.

When something goes wrong with your bread, odds are it isn't because the bread machine is messing up. It's more likely because you used too much or two little of a certain ingredient, like salt or yeast. If your bread consistently turns out poorly, however, no matter what you do, it's probably because of the machine.

Problem: Heavy/dense texture

<u>Solution</u>: Breads with a dense or heavy texture can be caused either by not enough of an ingredient or too much. Not enough sugar, yeast, water, or salt could be the cause, while too much flour, too many whole grains, or too many add-ins might also be to blame. Next time, be sure to measure very carefully. If you believe the flour is the problem and you're using whole-grain flour or whole grains, substitute half with regular bread flour. That can help lighten up the texture. If the bread has dried fruit or other add-ins, reduce how much you're using.

Problem: Doughy/gummy center

Solution: Finding out your bread has a gummy or doughy center or pockets is always disappointing. Too many wet or fatty ingredients like eggs, applesauce, and water is most likely the problem. Use less next time. Too much sugar could also be the reason, since sugar has a huge impact on the yeast activity. Make sure you aren't adding more than the recipe calls for or that you're using the wrong kind of yeast. For example, if the recipe calls for King Arthur's "brown yeast," that's what you need to use, because it's been formulated especially for lots of sugar. If you use regular yeast instead, odds are the sugar proportion will be out of whack.

If you believe your ingredients aren't to blame, it could be a problem with the baking conditions. If it's really cold, the loaf simply might not have gotten baked enough. While it's rarely the reason, your bread machine might actually be broken. If your bread is consistently doughy, no matter what you do, it's probably an issue with your machine.

Problem: Bread tastes rancid

Solution: Bread with a rancid taste is always caused by the ingredients. If you're using any whole-grain, like flour or wheat germ, they need to be stored in the fridge. If they're stored at room temp, they spoil quickly. Why? It has a higher fat content. White whole-wheat flour is made from the entire wheat berry, which has more fat. This means a shorter shelf life. To test if flour is rancid or not, eat a little. If it has a sour tang and stings your tongue, it's gone bad. Good whole-wheat flour will taste slightly nutty and there's no sting.

Bread with a sour and/or yeasty flavor is most likely caused by stale yeast or too much yeast. You'll know the difference, because bread with too much yeast will look quite different.

HOW TO STORE BREAD

Bread machine bread is so delicious, you might create more than you, your family, and your friends can eat in one sitting. Here are some tips for storing your bread machine creations:

Dough. After the kneading cycle, remove the dough from the machine. If you plan on using the dough within three days, you can store it in the refrigerator. Form the dough into a disk and place it in a sealable freezer bag, or store the dough in a lightly oiled bowl covered with plastic wrap. Yeast action will not stop in the refrigerator, so punch the dough down until it is completely chilled, and then once a day. When you are ready to bake bread, remove the dough from the refrigerator, shape it, let it rise, and bake. Bread machine dough has no preservatives, so freeze it if you aren't baking it in three days. Form the dough into a disk and place it in a sealable freezer bag. You can freeze bread dough for up to a month. When you are ready to bake the bread, remove the dough from the freezer, store it in the refrigerator overnight, shape it, let it rise, and bake. You can shape the dough into braids, loaves, knots, or other shapes before refrigerating or freezing it. Wrap the shapes tightly and store in the refrigerator (if you are baking within 24 hours) or the freezer. At the right time, unwrap the dough, allow it to rise at room temperature, and bake it.

Baked Bread. Once your baked bread is cooled, wrap the loaf in plastic wrap or a freezer bag and place it in the refrigerator or freezer. You can freeze baked bread for up to 6 months. To thaw the bread, remove it from the freezer, unwrap the loaf partially, and let it sit at room temperature. If you want to serve warm bread after refrigerating or freezing a loaf, wrap the bread in aluminum foil, and bake it in an oven preheated to 300°F for 10 to 15 minutes.

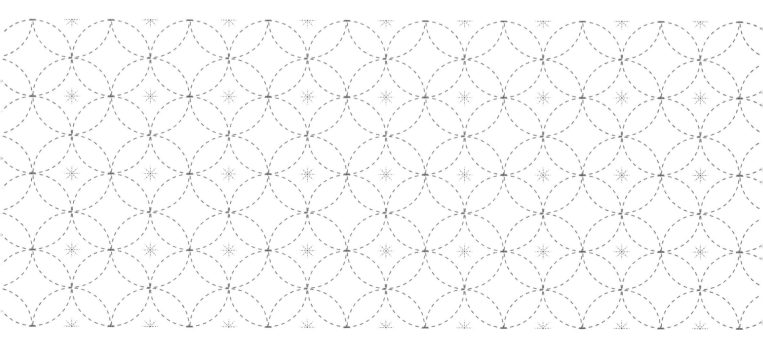

Storing the Leftover Bread

Top Storage Tips

Storing bread isn't always easy. If you manage not to eat all of the delicious goodies that you bake, you should find the best ways to store them so that you can keep them fresh longer. There are plenty of different things to keep in mind when it comes to storing bread, but homemade bread is especially delicate. Here are some tips to help you get the most out of your storage:

Don't store bread in the refrigerator. While this might seem like the freshness solution, it actually changes the alignment of the starch molecules, which is what causes bread to go stale. If you have leftovers from what you have baked, keep it on the counter or in the bread box.

Make sure that you don't leave bread sitting out for too long. Once you cut into a loaf, you have a limited amount of time to wrap it up and secure the freshness inside. If the interior is exposed to the air for too long, it will start to harden and go stale much quicker.

If your home or the bread itself is warm, do not put it in a plastic bag. The warmth will encourage condensation, which will prompt mold growth in the warm, moist environment. Wait until bread cools completely before storing it.

Pre-sliced and store-bought bread are going to go bad much quicker, simply because of all of the exposure and additives (which, ironically, are sometimes to retain freshness). If you're making your own bread with your bread machine, and you manage to have leftovers, these tips will make sure that you get the most out of your bread.

MEASUREMENT AND CONVERSION

3 teaspoons	1 tablespoon
2 tablespoons	1 ounce
4 tablespoons	¼ cup
8 tablespoons	½ cup
16 tablespoons	1 cup
2 cups	1 pint
4 cups	1 quart
4 quarts	1 gallon

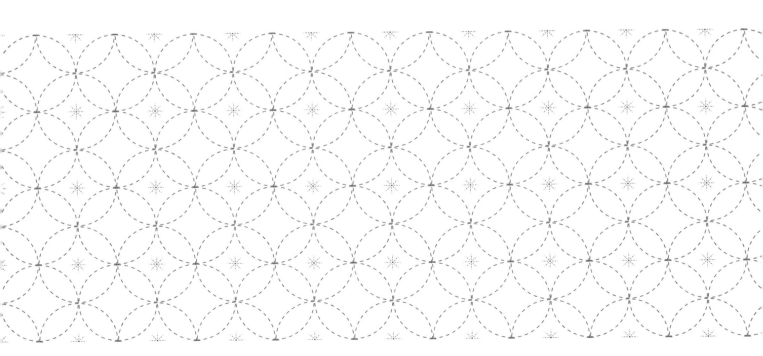

Type	Imperial	Imperial	Metric
Weight	1 dry ounce		28g
	1 pound	16 dry ounces	0.45 kg
Volume	1 teaspoon		5 ml
	1 dessert spoon	2 teaspoons	10 ml
	1 tablespoon	3 teaspoons	15 ml
	1 Australian tablespoon	4 teaspoons	20 ml
	1 fluid ounce	2 tablespoons	30 ml
	1 cup	16 tablespoons	240 ml
	1 cup	8 fluid ounces	240 ml
	1 pint	2 cups	470 ml
	1 quart	2 pints	0.95 l
	1 gallon	4 quarts	3.8 l
Length	1 inch		2.54 cm

* Numbers are rounded to the closest equivalent

Gluten-Free — Conversion Tables

All-Purpose Flour	Rice Flour	Potato Starch	Tapioca	Xanthan Gum
½ cup	1/3 cup	2 tablespoons	1 tablespoon	¼ teaspoon
1 cup	½ cup	3 tablespoons	1 tablespoon	½ teaspoon
¼ cup	¾ cup	1/3 cup	3 tablespoons	2/3 teaspoon
1 ½ cup	1 cup	5 tablespoons	3 tablespoons	2/3 teaspoon
1 ¾ cup	1 ¼ cup	5 tablespoons	3 tablespoons	1 teaspoon
2 cups	1 ½ cup	1/3 cup	1/3 cup	1 teaspoon
2 ½ cups	1 ½ cup	½ cup	¼ cup	1 1/8 teaspoon
2 2/3 cups	2 cups	½ cup	¼ cup	1 ¼ teaspoon
3 cups	2 cups	2/3 cup	1/3 cup	1 ½ cup

Flour: Quantity and Weight

Flour Amount
1 cup = 140 grams
3/4 cup = 105 grams
1/2 cup = 70 grams
1/4 cup = 35 grams

Cream: Quantity and Weight

Cream Amount
1 cup = 250 ml = 235 grams
3/4 cup = 188 ml = 175 grams
1/2 cup = 125 ml = 115 grams
1/4 cup = 63 ml = 60 grams
1 tablespoon = 15 ml = 15 grams

Sugar: Quantity and Weight

Sugar
1 cup = 200 grams
3/4 cup = 150 grams
2/3 cup = 135 grams
1/2 cup = 100 grams
1/3 cup = 70 grams
1/4 cup = 50 grams

Powdered Sugar
1 cup = 160 grams
3/4 cup = 120 grams
1/2 cup = 80 grams
1/4 cup = 40 grams

Butter: Quantity and Weight

Butter Amount
1 cup = 8 ounces = 2 sticks = 16 tablespoons =230 grams
1/2 cup = 4 ounces = 1 stick = 8 tablespoons = 115 grams
¼ cup = 2 ounces = ½ stick = 4 tablespoons= 58 grams

Oven Temperature Equivalent Chart

Fahrenheit (°F)	Celsius (°C)	Gas Mark
220	100	
225	110	1/4
250	120	1/2
275	140	1
300	150	2
325	160	3
350	180	4
375	190	5
400	200	6
425	220	7
450	230	8
475	250	9
500	260	

* Celsius (°C) = T (°F)−32] * 5/9
** Fahrenheit (°F) = T (°C) * 9/5 + 32
*** Numbers are rounded to the closest equivalent

CONCLUSION

This book has presented you with some of the easiest and delicious bread recipes you can find. One of the most mutual struggles for anyone following the diet is that they have to cut out so many of the foods they love, like sugary foods and starchy bread products. This book helps you overcome both those issues.

Focus your mindset toward the positive. Through a diet, you can help prevent diabetes, heart diseases, and respiratory problems. If you already feel pain from any of these, a diet under a doctor's supervision can greatly improve your condition.

These loaves of bread are made using the normal Ingredients you can find locally, so there's no need to have to order anything or have to go to any specialty stores for any of them. With these pieces of bread, you can enjoy the same meals you used to enjoy but stay on track with your diet as much as you want.

Lose the weight you want to lose, feel great, and still get to indulge in that piping hot piece of bread now and then. Spread on your favorite topping, and your bread craving will be satisfied.

Moreover, we have learned that the bread machine is a vital tool to have in our kitchen. It is not that hard to put into use. All you need to learn is how it functions and what its features are. You also need to use it more often to learn the dos and don'ts of using the machine.

The bread machine comes with a set of instructions that you must learn from the manual to use it the right way. There is a certain way of loading the Ingredients that must be followed, and the instructions

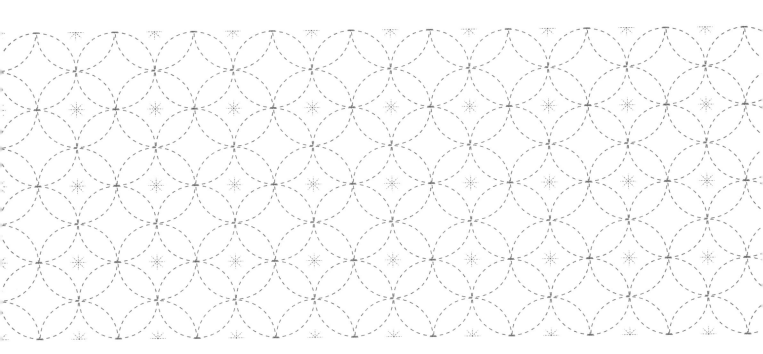

vary according to the make and the model. So, when you first get a machine, sit down and learn the manual from start to finish; this allows you to put it to good use and get better results. The manual will tell you exactly what to put in it, as well as the correct settings to use, according to the different ingredients and the type of bread you want to make.

Having a bread machine in your kitchen makes life easy. Whether you are a professional baker or a home cook, this appliance will help you get the best bread texture and flavors with minimum effort. Bread making is an art, and it takes extra care and special technique to deal with a specific type of flour and bread machine that enables you to do so even when you are not a professional. In this book, we have discussed all bread machines and how we can put them to good use. Basic information about flour and yeast is also discussed to give all the beginners an idea of how to deal with the major ingredients of bread and what variety to use to get a particular type of bread. And finally, some delicious bread recipes were shared so that you can try them at home!

Lightning Source UK Ltd.
Milton Keynes UK
UKHW050106110121
376714UK00006BA/460

9 781801 572347